Research Ideas for Young Scientists

RESEARCH IDEAS

FOR YOUNG SCIENTISTS

by George Barr

CONSULTANT IN ELEMENTARY SCIENCE,
BOARD OF EDUCATION, NEW YORK CITY

illustrated by John Teppich

WHITTLESEY HOUSE

McGraw-Hill Book Company, Inc.

New York   Toronto   London

FOURTH PRINTING

03802

Library of Congress Catalog Card Number: 58-12991

Published by Whittlesey House,
a division of the McGraw-Hill Book Company, Inc.

CONTENTS

The Human Body

Weather

Water

Insects

Plants

Introduction

This is a different kind of science book. It starts where other books end.

You will not be asked to repeat many experiments that have been done before. Instead, you will start on the exciting road to new experiments. You will then be in the same position as a research scientist when he is solving real mysteries.

You will be doing original experiments that concern the cold light of fireflies, the speed of ants, and whether your camera shutter is clicking accurately at one twenty-fifth of a second. You will build racing rockets; you will discover that dozens of iron objects in your home have mysteriously acquired magnetic north and south poles.

You will also find out whether or not cricket chirps can give us the temperature and if blindfolded people walk in circles.

No special laboratory will be needed to do the experiments. You will discover that in your own home you have an extremely accurate electric meter, chemical apparatus for extracting salt from the ocean, and even instruments for measuring split seconds!

This book will also help you in planning your own experiments to answer some questions you may dream up yourself.

What you discover will interest your friends and classmates too. It may even be suitable for presentation at your science club, science fairs, science assembly shows, and science contests.

This book includes a wide range of science topics. At the end of each section there are suggestions for further experimentation and reading.

You will learn the methods used by research scientists as you do your own experiments. You will thereby take a big step toward becoming a scientist yourself!

Making sure about things

Before you start your first experiment it is a good idea to consider what you have to do to get accurate results.

Always state your problem so clearly that you know exactly what you are looking for. Plan carefully, get good advice, and learn facts and techniques you may need for the experiment. If possible, work with an interested partner.

One of the best ways to make certain that everything is correct is to repeat the experiment many times. Test your results in every way. Think of possible sources of error. Invite your friends' criticism. Also, see if you get the same answers when you attack the problem in an entirely different way.

Always gather as much evidence as you can before you draw your final conclusions. It is unscientific to be satisfied with only one experiment.

Another important part of research work is to be able to make accurate comparisons before and after experimentation. Wherever possible you should have another setup just like the one on which you are working. All the conditions for both must be exactly the same except for the one thing that you are doing differently to the experimental one.

In this way you can compare one thing at a time and not have to guess about the reason for any change. This

USED
PLANT
FOOD **B**

USED
PLANT
FOOD **B**

USED
PLANT
FOOD **A**

CONTROL
NO PLANT FOOD

USED
PLANT
FOOD **A**

CONTROL
NO PLANT FOOD

kind of duplicate setup is called a *control,* and it is used in many experiments in this book.

For example, suppose you used a fertilizer on several plants and the plants grew very large. Could you honestly say that the fertilizer did it? Someone might say that the plants would have grown large without the fertilizer. But if you had several similar plants under the same conditions which did not receive the fertilizer you would have a better basis for comparison. The unfertilized plants are called controls.

ELECTRICITY AND MAGNETISM

Does your steam radiator have
a north and a south pole?

Bring a magnetic compass close to the top of a radiator in your home. You will probably find that the north end of the compass needle points to it.

Place the compass at the lower end of the radiator and the north end of the needle will swing away.

This shows that the radiator has two different poles and is therefore a magnet.

If you go through the house testing different iron objects you will become more and more excited at the number of weak magnets you have around you.

You have probably learned that iron objects become magnetized when they are near magnets. In this case, the earth is the magnet.

You will find that in order for these iron objects to have different poles on the top and bottom they must have been in one position for some time. In this way the iron in them is lined up in the earth's magnetic field.

You can devise many experiments that may occur to you. For example, a tin can of food from the pantry shows a north and south pole because it is about 98 per cent steel and has been in a vertical position for some time.

Turn the can over and test it daily. How long before it loses or changes its poles? Does a larger can take longer to change than a shorter one? If a can shows no poles, how long will it take for it to do so?

Here are some iron objects that may have north and south poles:

radiators   sinks (porcelain over iron)
floor lamps   bathtubs (porcelain over iron)
umbrellas in stands   wastepaper baskets
stoves   plates behind doorknobs
refrigerators   automobiles
metal table legs   gates and fences
alarm clocks   vertical steel columns
hinges on doors   in basement
electric switch plates   TV cabinets

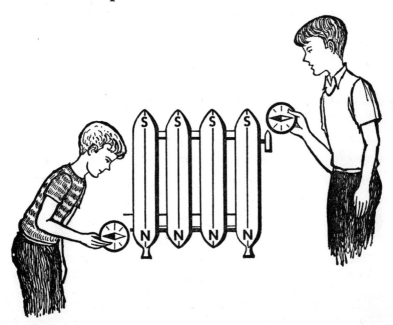

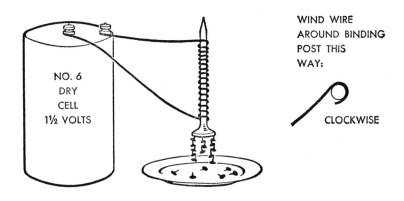

NO. 6
DRY
CELL
1½ VOLTS

WIND WIRE
AROUND BINDING
POST THIS
WAY:

CLOCKWISE

DRY CELLS IN SERIES

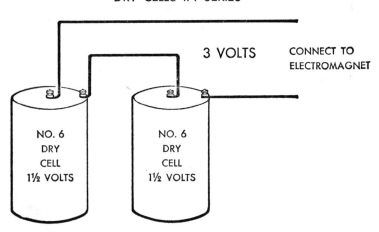

3 VOLTS

CONNECT TO
ELECTROMAGNET

NO. 6
DRY
CELL
1½ VOLTS

NO. 6
DRY
CELL
1½ VOLTS

How strong is your electromagnet?

You probably know how to make an electromagnet. Simply wind insulated wire around a nail. When the ends of the wire are connected to a source of electricity the nail will behave like a magnet.

You can test its strength by counting how many small nails it can pick up.

You will find that the more turns there are and the more electricity you use, the stronger the electromagnet will become.

However, your research problem is to find out whether an electromagnet becomes twice as strong when it has twice as many turns.

You will also learn whether the electromagnet is twice as strong when the source of electricity is doubled.

Use 18-gauge bell wire and make the turns around a 4-inch spike, starting at the head. Use the large (Number 6) dry cells.

Copy the chart on page 16 into your research notebook.

Complete it and study the findings.

Have you found that at a certain point the electromagnet stops getting stronger? Beyond that point the increase in strength does not keep in step with the number of turns of wire or the amount of electricity supplied to the wire.

You must remember, too, that the more turns you make, the less current will go through the wire.

Number of turns	Nails picked up by one dry cell	Nails picked up by two cells in series
3		
6		
9		
12		
15		
18		
21		
24		
27		
30		
33		
36		
60		

Watts in the house

It is useful to know how many watts an electrical device uses, because then you can find the cost of operating it. You can also learn whether a circuit is being overloaded and is in danger of "blowing" a fuse.

Most pieces of electrical equipment have manufacturers' plates on them that give the wattage. However, if this plate is not present you can use the regular electric meter to help you find the information. This meter is usually in the basement or outside the building.

In addition to the clocklike dials in the meter, there is a spinning disk that is pivoted between the poles of magnets. It goes around and around when electricity is being used in the house.

This circular aluminum disk has a black spot painted on its edge so you can tell when it makes one revolution.

The more electricity you use, the faster this disk turns. But what is more interesting is that the speed corresponds to the number of watts used. In other words, it will spin five times as fast for 500 watts as for 100 watts.

To start the test, see that no electrical device is operating in your house. If the refrigerator, oil burner, or air conditioner starts up while you are making a reading, disregard your results and wait until it goes off. Perhaps your parents will not mind shutting them off for a very short time.

Since electric clocks use only 2 watts, they will hardly

affect your figures unless you have several in the house.

Now place a 100-watt bulb in a socket and note how many seconds it takes for the black spot to come around five times. Remove the 100-watt bulb and plug the device with the unknown wattage into any outlet in the house. Again, count the seconds for five turns.

If the unknown device makes the disk turn twice as fast as before, then it is using two times as much electricity. It is therefore a 200-watt appliance.

If the disk turns twenty times as fast as it did for the 100-watt bulb, it is consuming twenty times as much electricity, or 2,000 watts.

On the other hand, if the disk turns half as fast as for the 100-watt bulb, then you have a 50-watt device.

By estimation you can get fairly accurate results.

It is a good idea to work with a friend who does the timing while you watch the turning.

Use a flashlight when you are in the basement. This is not a dangerous experiment, but just to be on the safe side, make sure all the fuse boxes are closed. Do not touch anything near the meter box.

By the way, do all the 100-watt bulbs you have in the house make the disk turn at the same rate? Try testing them. The results may surprise you.

Make a chart in your research notebook like the one shown on page 20.

Fill in the number of seconds needed for five turns of the disk when each device is plugged in separately.

Figure out the wattage.

Compare this with the wattage printed on the device.

Device	Number of seconds for five turns	Calculated wattage	Wattage printed on device
100-watt bulb			
Small radio			
Large radio			
Television set			
Electric fan			
Small record player			
Toaster			
Electric iron			
Sewing machine			
Electric shaver			
Refrigerator			
Broiler			
Electric drill			
Vacuum cleaner			
Unknown wattage device			

More to find out:

How much electricity is used in your house?

It is easy to read the electric meter. It has four dials. To read it, start with the left dial. Write down the number that the indicator passed last. Do the same for the

METER READS 6705 KILOWATT HOURS

other three dials. The number of kilowatt-hours is the number obtained when all four figures are written together. For example, the dials may read 6705. If next week the new reading is 6805, then 100 kilowatt-hours have been consumed. Make graphs showing how much is used daily for a week.

Is the north pole of a magnet as strong as the south pole?

Devise an accurate and convincing test. HINT: See how many tacks are picked up by each end.

Can you magnetize recording tape?

If you own or can borrow a tape recorder you can do some experiments. The plastic recording tape contains iron particles which can be arranged in certain positions in the tape during the recording process. Try to pick up recording tape with a magnet. You might also try to magnetize a 1-inch separate piece of tape by rubbing one end of it with one end of a magnet. Now test whether both ends of this small strip are equally attracted to the same end of a magnet.

Can you demagnetize a needle?

First magnetize a needle by rubbing one pole of a magnet a few times over the same end of the needle. Rub in only one direction. Test the magnetism by picking up small iron clips. You can destroy the magnetism by heating the needle in a gas flame until it is red hot. (Careful! Use pliers to hold it.) Banging the needle with a hammer or rubbing its poles with a magnet may demagnetize it too.

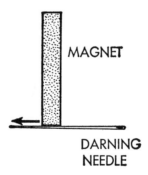

MAGNET

DARNING
NEEDLE

What you are doing is causing the orderly arrangement of the iron particles to become disarranged. This ruins the magnetism.

What is the best day for static electricity experiments?

Blow up a balloon and tie its mouth. Rub it ten times with a woolen cloth. Place it on the wall. Record how long it stays there. Do it a few times to get the average time. Duplicate the conditions and try it on humid days and on dry days.

Will a magnet pick up a Canadian nickel?

An American 5-cent piece has less nickel in it than a Canadian one. Nickel is a magnetic substance. HINT: Pure nickel is a magnetic metal. Nickel coins, however, contain copper too. United States nickels have less nickel in them than Canadian ones and are therefore less magnetic.

Books to read

Nelson Beeler and Franklyn Branley, *Experiments with Electricity,* New York: Thomas Y. Crowell Company, 1947.

Jeanne Bendick, *Electronics for Young People,* New York: Whittlesey House, 1955.

S. R. Cook, *Electrical Things Boys Like to Make,* Milwaukee: The Bruce Publishing Company, 1954.

Jack Gould, *All About Radio and Television,* New York: Random House, Inc., 1953.

Alfred P. Morgan, *Boy's First Book of Radio and Electronics,* New York: Charles Scribner's Sons, 1954.

———, *First Electrical Book for Boys,* New York: Charles Scribner's Sons, 1951.

Herman and Nina Schneider, *More Power to You,* New York: William R. Scott, Inc., 1956.

R. F. Yates, *The Boys' Book of Magnetism,* New York: Harper and Brothers, 1941.

———, *A Boy and a Motor,* New York: Harper and Brothers, 1944.

TRANSPORTATION

How many miles on a
gallon of gasoline?

This is a useful bit of information for your father to know because it gives him an idea of the condition of the car. It also helps him find the cost of a trip he is planning.

Start the test by having the gas tank filled up to the brim while the car is on level ground. It is a good idea to shake the car to remove any air bubbles from the tank.

Copy down the mileage and thereafter keep a record of all the gasoline the tank has added to it. It is not necessary to fill up to the top every time. Continue until at least thirty gallons have been consumed. Of course, the more gasoline you use before ending your test, the more accurate will be the results.

Try to use the same brand of gas and to do just one kind of driving, such as in city traffic or on open highways.

When you are ready to end your test, have the tank filled right up to the brim, again on a level spot. Shake the car as before.

Subtracting the starting mileage from the present

mileage will give you the number of miles traveled during the test.

The number of gallons of gas used is what was added during the test, including the amount needed at the end to bring the tank to its original full condition. Here is a sample test:

Date: June 15 to July 12
Type of driving: City traffic
Miles at end: 20,396.9
Miles at start: 19,652.4
Miles traveled: 744.5
Gallons of gas used: $12 + 6 + 9 + 14 + 10 + 9.4 =$
                                                          60.4 gallons

$$Miles\ per\ gallon = \frac{Miles\ traveled\ (744.5)}{Gallons\ used\ (60.4)}$$
$$= 12.3 \text{ miles per gallon}$$

Try to answer these questions:

1. Is there a difference between high-test and regular gas, as far as gas consumption is concerned?
2. Can you save money by overinflating tires by three pounds?
3. Do you actually save money by installing new spark plugs or having a motor tune-up?

More things to do:

1. Ask a new-car dealer to show you the quick method he uses to check gas consumption.
2. Ask new-car dealers about the yearly Gas Economy

Run contests for experts who get fabulous mileages by special techniques.

3. Ask drivers of heavy trucks what mileage they get on a gallon of gas.
4. Find out about gas records for outboard motors, motorboats, scooters, and airplanes.

Flight testing homemade rocket balloons

Do you know what makes a jet airplane swish through the air or a rocket hurtle through space? A huge amount of gas is being forced out through the back opening of the plane or rocket. This makes it go forward because of a principle stated by Sir Isaac Newton over two hundred years ago—long before there were jet planes!

He said that for every action there is an equal and opposite reaction. To demonstrate this, blow up a balloon and let it go. It will jump out of your hand and zig-zag around the room. Its direction is always opposite to the flow of air out of the balloon.

In order to make the balloon go in a straight line, insert a paper tube in its mouth and suspend it by strings from a wire.

The tube that goes into the mouth before the string is tied around it is very important. By pinching the tube you can make it act like a valve to control the rate at which the air escapes.

The tube is made by wrapping a piece of stiff paper, such as a post card, around a pencil. Scotch tape or string will prevent the tube from unwinding. Clear nail

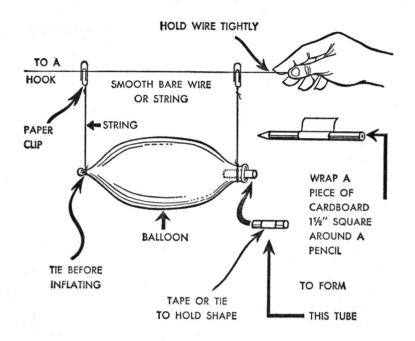

HOLD WIRE TIGHTLY

TO A HOOK

SMOOTH BARE WIRE OR STRING

PAPER CLIP

STRING

WRAP A PIECE OF CARDBOARD 1½" SQUARE AROUND A PENCIL

BALLOON

TIE BEFORE INFLATING

TAPE OR TIE TO HOLD SHAPE

TO FORM THIS TUBE

polish can be used to give it stiffness and make it water-proof.

The paper clips are hooked over the wire and the strings adjusted so that the top of the inflated balloon does not rub against the wire. Strings which are too long will cause the balloon to flop around. When properly adjusted, the balloon should be parallel to the wire.

Suggestions

If the inflated balloon does not budge, press the tube open or make a larger tube.

The best wire to use is 22-gauge bare copper wire. Avoid kinking it.

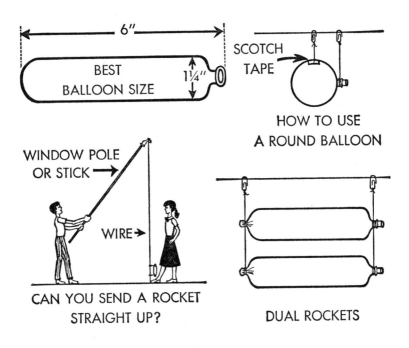

|←——— 6" ———→|

BEST BALLOON SIZE 1¼"

SCOTCH TAPE

HOW TO USE A ROUND BALLOON

WINDOW POLE OR STICK →

WIRE →

CAN YOU SEND A ROCKET STRAIGHT UP?

DUAL ROCKETS

Have races with your friends by using two wires next to each other.

See how far you can send a balloon. Twenty-five feet is an average distance.

The big secret is to use the type of balloon shown in the illustration.

How far did your helium balloon travel?

When you were small, did you ever accidentally let go of a helium-filled balloon, and then watch it rise and drift out of sight? You surely must have wondered how far it went.

People sometimes enclose their names and addresses in bottles and throw them into the ocean. It is exciting to receive a reply months and even years later. Ocean currents have also been studied this way.

You can have the same thrill by releasing a number of helium-filled balloons to each of which is tied a light waterproof plastic bag containing a self-addressed postal card and note for the finder.

You can share the expense with a few friends. Perhaps everyone in your class in school may wish to send one up. You have a much better chance of getting replies if thirty balloons are sent up.

Study the wind direction high up in the sky by observing the clouds. You must wait for a favorable breeze

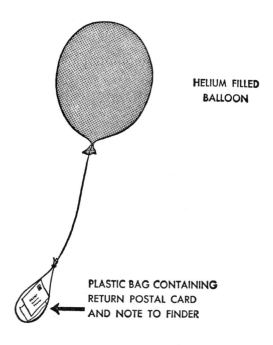

HELIUM FILLED
BALLOON

PLASTIC BAG CONTAINING
RETURN POSTAL CARD
AND NOTE TO FINDER

if you wish the balloon to drift in a certain direction, away from the ocean, forest, or mountain.

Most balloons probably do not land unbroken. Even those sent up by the Weather Bureau will expand as they rise. They finally burst because of the reduced air pressure in the upper air.

Of course, the best thing to do to insure getting returns is to have a group of your friends buy about a hundred inexpensive balloons. Fill them from a helium cylinder a high-school chemistry teacher has or knows where to buy. You might also try getting reduced prices in some toyshop that has a large cylinder and will fill the balloons for you.

The note might have the following information:

To the Finder

This plastic bag was sent up in a helium-filled balloon on March 22, 1959, by Elsa Dean, 135 Jackson Avenue, Laurelton 13, New York.

Will you please return the self-addressed postal card? In the interest of science kindly write when and where you found the plastic bag. If you will include your name and address I shall be happy to send you a report of all the replies I receive.

Elsa Dean

What accounts for the force of a collision?

The force of any collision depends mainly upon the speed and the weight of the moving object.

You can prove this yourself by using your table top as the testing grounds.

To make the test, roll something down to a block of wood or a box or any other target and measure the distance this object is pushed back. The rolling objects will be light, medium weight, and heavy. The speeds will be slow, moderate, and fast.

These speeds will be caused by the tilt of the table as you place different numbers of books under one side.

The ordinary tin can makes a good rolling object. Use an empty one, a light unopened one, and another unopened but heavier one.

Place a pile of books 5 inches high under the legs on one side of a table and allow the lightweight can to roll toward the target whose position has been marked. Measure the distance it was moved when it was hit. Do the same for the other two cans.

Placing more books under the table legs will give the cans more speed for the other tests.

Instead of the cans you may wish to use a toy truck or a roller skate. Their weights can be increased by adding stones or tying on some objects.

From your results you will learn that the heavier a moving object is, and the faster it moves, the more damage it can inflict.

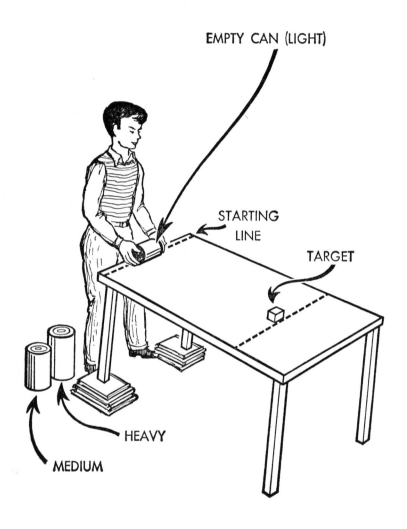

EMPTY CAN (LIGHT)

STARTING LINE

TARGET

HEAVY

MEDIUM

Actually, a light object can have a great deal of impact if it is moving fast. That is why a bullet has such force.

A heavy object, on the other hand, can produce violent wrecks even if it is going slowly. A very slow-moving ship can cut another one in two.

These effects are due to *momentum*. A moving object's momentum is calculated by multiplying its speed by its weight. That is why the momentum of a heavy object moving slowly can be as great as that of a lighter object traveling fast.

	Moving object	Number of inches target was moved
Slow speed	Light weight	
	Medium weight	
	Heavy weight	
Moderate speed	Light weight	
	Medium weight	
	Heavy weight	
Fast speed	Light weight	
	Medium weight	
	Heavy weight	

More to find out:

How quickly can you stop your bicycle?

Test your reaction time and brakes by having a friend decide where and when to call STOP as you ride by. Measure the distance covered before you come to a stop. Make a chart for slow, medium, and fast speeds.

Why is it easy to go up a ramp?

Tie a rubber band to a skate. Measure the stretch needed to lift the skate vertically to a chair. Now obtain a board and make a ramp from the floor to the chair. See how much stretch is needed to move the skate from the floor to the chair using the ramp. Try a longer ramp. Chart the distance and the stretch.

What is the traffic picture at a busy corner?

Make a survey by counting the number of cars and pedestrians during certain hours. Make charts for all directions and turns.

Here is a sample chart.

TRAFFIC AT FRONT AND FIRST AVENUES				
Date: ——— Time	Number of cars coming from the			
	North	South	East	West
p.m. 4:45–5:00				
5:00–5:15				
5:15–5:30				

Why are ships pointed?

Cut a few pieces of thin wood into rectangles 2 inches by 4 inches. Now cut a point on one, round the narrow end of another, and leave one as it is. Place them in

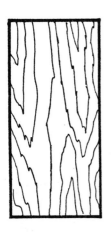  

water in a sink or tub and give all the same push forward by means of a stick held against the backs of all. Which went farthest? Try different kinds of points.

Does a ship float higher in salt or fresh water?

Stick a thumbtack into the eraser of a pencil. When placed in water this way, the pencil will float with its point above water. Mark how high it floats in tap water. Now add different amounts of salt and mark the pencil each time. You can also add sand to a small vial so that it just about sinks in fresh water but it will float in a strong salt solution.

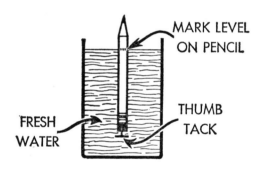

MARK LEVEL ON PENCIL

THUMB TACK

FRESH WATER

Why does a bicycle help us travel fast?

Measure how much distance the rear wheel moves along the ground when the pedals make one complete turn. Count the number of teeth on the large sprocket wheel of the pedals and also on the smaller sprocket wheel of the rear wheel.

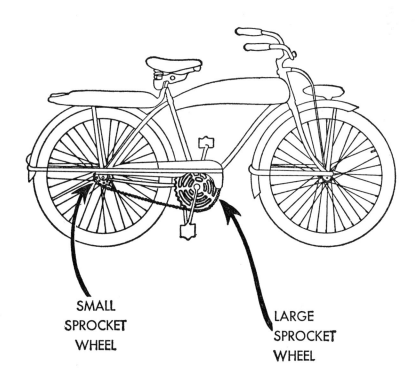

SMALL
SPROCKET
WHEEL

LARGE
SPROCKET
WHEEL

Books to read

Franklyn Branley, *Experiments in the Principles of Space Travel*, New York: Thomas Y. Crowell Company, 1955.

Edward G. Huey, *What Makes the Wheels Go Round*, New York: Harcourt, Brace and Company, Inc., 1952.

Margaret O. Hyde, *Flight Today and Tomorrow*, New York: Whittlesey House, 1958.

F. C. Lane, *All About Rockets and Jets,* New York: Random House, Inc., 1954.

John B. Lewellen, *The Atomic Submarine,* New York: Thomas Y. Crowell Company, 1954.

————, *You and American Life Lines; a Story of Transportation,* Chicago: Children's Press, 1952.

Willy Ley, *Rockets, Missiles, and Space Travel,* New York: The Viking Press, Inc., 1957.

Lynn Poole, *Your Trip into Space,* New York: Whittlesey House, 1958.

Leo Schneider and M. U. Ames, *Wings in Your Future,* New York: Harcourt, Brace and Company, Inc., 1955.

SOUND AND LIGHT

What is the best way to make a string telephone?

Have you ever made a string telephone? Most of us have made many. Each time we used another kind of string. We also changed the cans. Some worked better than others.

Good systematic research ought to teach you which materials are best. Most of the time we try too many things at one time, so that we really do not know what is responsible for the improvement.

People frequently suggest using waxed shoemaker's thread. Use that, and also try different types of ordinary string, nylon fishing line, upholsterer's thread, strong carpet or button thread, and other things you may have at home. Have you ever used various sizes of copper or iron wire?

The method of attaching the string to the can should be important. Try knots, buttons, glue, sealing wax, or metal washers. Instead of using one hole, tie the string through two holes.

Make sure the string is tight. We know that a loose line is no good, but is it possible to pull the string so tightly that the can refuses to vibrate?

Maybe the secret lies mainly in the cans you use. Try metal cans that are large, medium, small, deep, and shallow. Experiment with cut-down paper milk-containers of all sizes. Look around for those stiff paper drinking cups with handles, used for hot liquids. They may produce excellent sounds.

In order to compare the sounds you receive, you must always have the same loudness at the sending end. It may be difficult to control the voice, so use a loudly ticking clock, or a buzzer, or a record player set at the same volume for each test.

Because of the many different things that can change in this experiment, you will probably be able to discover only those features that make a big difference in the quality of the string telephone.

For example, how can you tell if the string is exactly as tight as in a previous test? Also, are you sure you can remember how loudly you heard the last test?

Of course, scientists have special instruments to determine these things accurately, but you can still get good results with this research by using careful judgment.

How far can the ground carry sound?

You have seen movies of Indians with their ears to the ground, listening for the approaching enemy. Since this is usually done in broad daylight, and on open prairies, we are supposed to believe that the Indian is hearing farther than he can see.

So, once and for all, let us get to the bottom of this. Can we hear this way for over a mile, or just half a mile, or only two hundred yards?

Do this research with a friend. Find a small rock that is partly underground and strike it with another one

while your friend has his ear to the ground a small distance away. He keeps going farther away until he cannot hear the thumps any longer.

The distance can be measured by counting the number of paces. Determine the length of your stride by getting an average of many steps.

You can also bang a wooden or metal fence which is in the ground.

Does the ground carry the sound better than the air? Does the nature of the ground make a difference—grassy, hard-packed road, marshy, sandy?

The Indians used to put their teeth on their knives stuck into the ground. How much does that improve reception? Use a butter spreader or a dull knife.

How reliable is your camera's shutter?

Have you been getting poor snapshots lately, even though you used the recommended exposure?

Maybe your shutter speed is not what it is supposed to be.

How does one go about testing 1/25 second or 1/50 second?

There are complicated professional methods, of course. Perhaps you can think of a simple, sure-fire test. Can you do better than the one that is given here?

If you place something on a phonograph turntable and photograph it while it is whirling around, you will get a blur. The angle of the blur can be measured and the shutter speed calculated.

The next time you use a roll of film, save your last shot for this test. Take a record player, with an extension cord, out into the bright sunlight. Use the standard 78-rpm (revolutions per minute) speed.

Place a 10- or 12-inch record on the turntable. Tape a thin white paper strip to the record from the center to the edge.

Hold the camera vertically over it. Look into the finder and snap while the record is turning. Get the picture of the turntable as large as possible but keep the camera focused.

When the picture is printed, measure the angle with a protractor—or compare it with the one shown in the diagram.

It is a good idea to find out first if your phonograph's 78-rpm speed is correct. Make a mark of some kind on the turntable and count the revolutions in one minute.

The mathematics is given in case you wish to know how to work out any further problems.

Each revolution $= 360$ degrees.

$360 \times 78 =$ the total number of degrees turned in one minute.

If you divide this by 60 you get the number of degrees turned in one second.

$\dfrac{360 \times 78}{60} = 468$ degrees in one second.

In 1/25 second, the angle of the blur should be $\dfrac{468}{25}$, which is about 19 degrees.

WHITE STRIP

78 REVOLUTIONS PER MINUTE

For 1/50 second it is $\frac{468}{50}$, which is about 9 degrees.

For 1/100 second it is $\frac{468}{100}$, which is about 5 degrees.

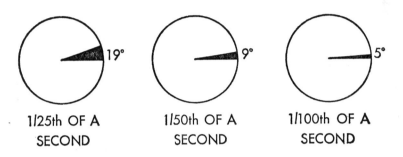

1/25th OF A SECOND

1/50th OF A SECOND

1/100th OF A SECOND

WHAT THE PHOTOGRAPH SHOULD LOOK LIKE
IF THE SHUTTER SPEED IS CORRECT

How much does a lens magnify?

There may be times when you wish to know exactly how great is the magnification of a lens, a telescope, a pair of opera glasses, or a pair of binoculars.

To find out how many times a lens enlarges, get into focus the lines of a ruled piece of paper. Notice the lines outside the lens and the lines under the lens and compare. Count how many spaces of the page seen outside the lens will go into one enlarged space seen through the lens. (See the illustration on page 49.)

To learn the power of binoculars or opera glasses hold the glasses in the right hand. With the right eye held to the left lens, focus on a brick wall. The left eye, being free, will get an image of the bricks also. Do not stand too far away to see them clearly.

You will find that your eyes will combine both the magnified and unmagnified images so that one will be seen over the other.

The number of rows of unmagnified bricks that you can place in one enlarged brick is the magnification.

Measure the enlarging powers of drinking glasses or jars filled with water by holding the ruled paper behind them. Sometimes you may have to move the paper away from the object for a short distance to get the greatest enlargement.

Also try a soda-pop bottle, a glass or clear plastic stirring rod, a gallon jug, a piece of clear glass, a marble, a large clear plastic cookie container. Fill all containers with water first.

Make a lens by placing a drop of water on waxed paper; hold it over a newspaper and see how it enlarges the print. To measure magnification hold it over the fine double lines found around an advertisement. Compare the enlarged lines with the others.

If a drop of water is placed on a piece of glass or clear plastic, it can be raised from the newspaper and may give a higher magnification.

Build a waterdrop lens by first making a loop at the end of a length of fine wire. Dip the loop into water. See how many times the waterdrop which is formed there will enlarge.

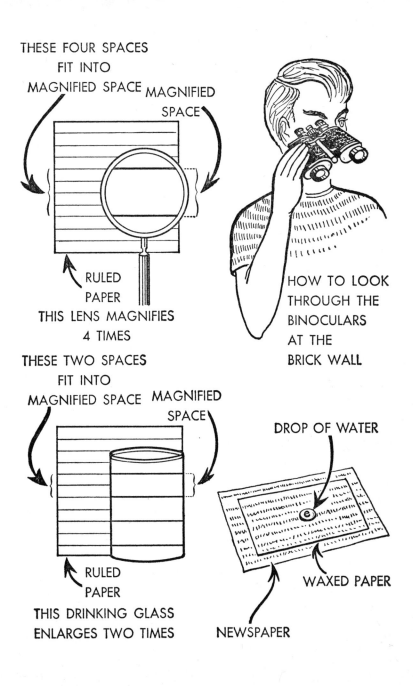

THESE FOUR SPACES
FIT INTO
MAGNIFIED SPACE MAGNIFIED
SPACE

RULED
PAPER
THIS LENS MAGNIFIES
4 TIMES

HOW TO LOOK
THROUGH THE
BINOCULARS
AT THE
BRICK WALL

THESE TWO SPACES
FIT INTO
MAGNIFIED SPACE MAGNIFIED
SPACE

DROP OF WATER

RULED
PAPER
THIS DRINKING GLASS
ENLARGES TWO TIMES

WAXED PAPER

NEWSPAPER

Object	Enlargement
Hand lens	4✕
Gallon jug	2✕
Juice glass	
Waterdrop on wire	
Waterdrop on glass	
6-inch cookie jar	
Marble	
³⁄₁₆-inch glass stirrer	
Cheap telescope	
Opera glasses	
Dad's eyeglasses	

More to find out:

Can you measure the speed of sound?

Look toward a factory steam whistle at noon or at quitting time. Carefully use a tape measure to find your distance, or get it from a town map. Count seconds after you see the blast until you hear the sound.

Can you hear as well with your right ear as you can with your left?

Devise an accurate test using an alarm clock.

Close one ear and find out how far away your open ear can hear the ticking of the alarm clock.

Is there a "dead" spot in your school auditorium?

Plug in a record player on the stage and listen to it as you walk around to every section of the auditorium. You may find that there are places where the sound is very poor. How can you remedy this condition? Does facing the loudspeaker of the record player in another direction help?

Can you make an ice "burning glass"?

Try to get a clear convex lens by freezing water in a smooth saucer. Hold the edge of the ice lens with a towel and focus the sun's rays on tissue paper.

Can you get tired of seeing red?

Stare at a square piece of red paper for about a minute. Then look at a white paper and you will see a blue-green square. This is because the nerve endings in your eyes that see red get tired and do not respond to red. Now, white paper is white because it reflects all the colors: red, orange, yellow, green, blue, violet. In this case your eye sees all but the red. This accounts for the blue-green *afterimage*, as it is called. Make a chart recording the afterimages of other colors you look at.

Can you make a telescope?

Get two lenses, one with a long focal length and the other with a shorter one. The focal length is the distance from the lens to the image it makes. Look at some distant object through both lenses at the same time but keep the lens with the shorter focal length closer to your eye. The image will be upside down. Experiment to get the best results. Put the lenses in a cardboard tube.

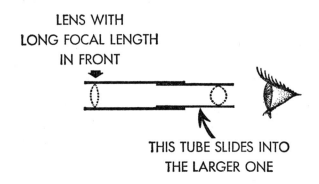

LENS WITH
LONG FOCAL LENGTH
IN FRONT

THIS TUBE SLIDES INTO
THE LARGER ONE

Books to read

Irving Adler, *Secret of Light,* New York: International Press, 1952.

Marion E. Baer, *Sound: An Experiment Book,* New York: Holiday House, Inc., 1952.

J. F. Batchelor, *Communication from Cave Writing to Television,* New York: Harcourt, Brace and Company, Inc., 1953.

Nelson E. Beeler and Franklyn M. Branley, *Experiments*

with a Microscope, New York: Thomas Y. Crowell Company, 1957.

Ira and May Freeman, *Fun with Your Camera,* New York: Random House, Inc., 1955.

John Hoke, *The First Book of Photography,* New York: Franklin Watts, Inc., 1954.

Larry Kettlekamp, *The Magic of Sound,* New York: William Morrow and Company, Inc., 1956.

Julius Schwartz, *Through the Magnifying Glass,* New York: Whittlesey House, 1954.

THE HUMAN BODY

Who has the largest lung capacity?

Fill a gallon jug with water. Place your palm over its mouth and turn it upside down in a basin of water. Remove your hand. Now insert the end of a 2-foot rubber hose into the jug.

When you blow into the tube some water is blown out of the jug. You can tell which of your friends has the largest lung capacity by observing the level of the water in the bottle after each try. Tape a ruler to the outside of the bottle. Before you make your try, it is permissible to inhale deeply several times, but all the air you blow into the tube should be blown in after one breath and before the next breath.

The end of the hose that you blow into can be kept sanitary by inserting a clean plastic tube into it after each person's try.

If you want to know the actual volume of water you displaced, put your palm under the mouth of the jug and turn it over. Measure how much water you must add to fill the bottle.

Do you think this test shows how much air you have in your lungs? Do you think you really blow every last bit of air from your lungs? No, you do not. There is still a large amount of air left in the lungs. At any rate, you have a way of comparing your lung capacities.

Does a person with the best blowing ability have the largest chest expansion? Use a tape measure to measure the chest size before a deep breath and after it. The difference in inches is called the *chest expansion.*

RULER TAPED TO GLASS
LOW NUMBERS ON TOP

RUBBER HOSE

CLEAN PLASTIC
TUBE

Can you increase your capacity by breathing in and out rapidly for a few moments before you are tested? Can you think of any other way?

Instead of trying for a record, just breathe out through the pipe and in through your nose. Do this at your normal rate for one minute. Multiply by 60 the volume you displaced in one minute and you will know the amount you exhale (or inhale) in an hour. Calculate how much air you exhale in a day or in a seventy-year lifetime.

Repeat this last activity after you run around for five minutes. You will learn how much more air you use when you exert yourself if you again measure the amount you exhale in one minute.

What is your body temperature during the day?

Warm-blooded living things are supposed to have an even temperature except, of course, when there is illness. The normal body temperature is 98.6° Fahrenheit, but many of us may vary slightly from this and still be in perfect health.

A less well-known fact is that our temperature changes during the day. Every person has his own type of variation. It should be a very interesting bit of information to make a graph of your body temperature during the day.

Always shake the thermometer down to the lowest reading before using it. Clean with cold water.

Place the bulb of the thermometer under the tongue for about two minutes. Here it is warmed by an ample blood supply. Keep it in place with your lips and not with your teeth. Do not talk. You should not use a mouth thermometer for about twenty minutes after eating or drinking something cold or warm.

Most people have their lowest temperature about 6 A.M. and their highest at about 6 P.M.

Take your temperature when you get up and every two hours from then on, so that you can graph a complete day. See if you get the same curve on different days.

The next time you get a fever, keep yourself occupied

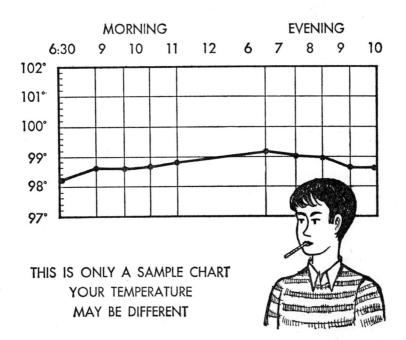

THIS IS ONLY A SAMPLE CHART
YOUR TEMPERATURE
MAY BE DIFFERENT

by making a very accurate temperature graph. See if it follows your daily pattern.

Copy this chart in your research notebook and fill in as many of the temperature readings as you can. Naturally, all these readings could not be taken in one day.

Activity	Temperatures	
	Before	After
Breakfast		
Lunch		
Supper		
Twenty minutes after cold drink of water		
Afternoon nap		
Fast bicycle ride		
Basketball practice		
Fast, long walk		
Cold shower		
Ten minutes after hot bath		
Sun bathing		
Fifteen minutes after being out in freezing weather when you feel chilled		
When you feel very warm		

Does a blindfolded person walk in a circle?

People who have been lost in the woods report that even though they thought they were walking in one direction they found themselves back in the same place they started from. Apparently, they had walked in a circle.

Is there something in our brain which makes us do this? Can we prevent it from happening?

For this experiment you should choose a very large, level, unobstructed area such as a smooth lawn in a park or a huge unused parking lot.

Blindfold a friend and direct him to go toward a spot about three hundred yards away. Avoid the possibility of his being influenced by sounds of people, automobiles, or animals. Perhaps you can have him wear ear muffs or plug his ears with absorbent cotton.

Walk a short distance behind him. Trace his path as accurately as you can on a large piece of paper or use chalk on the pavement, if possible.

Try it with various friends. Find out if they all have the same pattern.

If a person always turns in one direction, can he be prevented from doing this on another trial if he turns his head slightly in the opposite direction? Can he try consciously to avoid making the error?

Do not work on this experiment in any place where there is even a remote possibility of an automobile's approaching.

More to find out:

How many calories do you consume
a day?

The table given below shows the average need of
boys and girls. Get a library book giving the number of
calories in average servings of foods. Make a chart listing each food you eat in one day, the quantities, and the
calories.

Age	Boys	Girls
10	2,400	2,200
11	2,450	2,250
12	2,500	2,300
13	2,750	2,350
14	3,000	2,400
15	3,200	2,450
16	3,300	2,475

How fast do our muscles get tired?

Make a fist with your right hand then open it completely. Continue doing this as rapidly as possible until you are too tired to open your hand once more. Record the number of times. Wait one minute and do it again. Repeat this procedure many times. Of course, each time you can do it fewer times. Chart the results and study them. Compare with your friends.

RESULTS OF FATIGUE TEST									
Trial number	1	2	3	4	5	6	7	8	etc.
Number of fists made									

What did you inherit from your relatives?

Red hair, dimples, shape of ear lobes, turned-up nose, baldness, color of skin, moles, shape of fingers, hairy arms—these are some of the things that seem to run in families. Make out a card for one of the special features that you have. Do a great deal of investigating and find out who else among your relatives has this trait. See how many generations you can go back.

How fast does your "motor" calm down?

Take your normal pulse, then run or do something to speed it up. Record how long it takes to get it back to normal. Is there something you can do to slow down your pulse more quickly? Try drinking a warm drink, lying flat on your back, closing your eyes, or raising your legs on a pillow while you are in bed. Can your mind slow down your heartbeat? Try concentrating on a peaceful country scene. Make a graph showing the time it takes to get back to normal.

Which eye does most of the work?

Eye doctors say that one eye is usually more alert than the other. To test which is the favorite, hold a finger up at arm's length. With both eyes open look past it at a distant object. Now close the right eye. If the finger appears to jump to the right, then it is your right eye that you use more.

How fast does a baby breathe?

The breathing rate of an adult is about fourteen times a minute. Up to age five the rate may be three times faster. Count the chest movements of a number of sleeping children. Compare with adults at rest.

What is in most cough drops?

Make a list of the ingredients found on the boxes of about a dozen kinds of cough drops. Make a chart showing the number of times each ingredient is used. Ask your druggist the purpose of those in cough drops.

How fast does your hair grow?

Cut or shave the hair away from an area on your arm. Leave just one lonely hair. Can you think of any other ways of measuring hair growth?

Books to read

M. L. Cosgrave, *The Wonders Inside You,* New York: Dodd, Mead & Company, Inc., 1955.

John Perry, *Our Wonderful Eyes,* New York: Whittlesey House, 1955.

Anthony Ravielli, *Wonders of the Human Body,* New York: The Viking Press, Inc., 1954.

Herman and Nina Schneider, *How Your Body Works,* New York: William R. Scott, Inc., 1949.

Leo Schneider, *You and Your Senses,* New York: Harcourt, Brace and Company, Inc., 1956.

Herbert S. Zim, *Our Senses and How They Work,* New York: William Morrow & Company, Inc., 1956.

WEATHER

How accurate is the weather bureau?

The weatherman certainly takes a great deal of abuse from people. Yet he claims that he is about 85 per cent accurate.

He says that he gets into trouble when he considers many complicated things and then has to give a one-word prediction such as *Rain, Fair,* or *Warmer*.

Can you devise a test of the accuracy of the official weather prediction? Include temperature, precipitation, wind speed and direction, sky condition, and overall one-word predictions. Do it for a few weeks.

Make up your mind before you start what should be considered wrong. For example, if 78 degrees was predicted and 77 degrees is the actual temperature, it would not be fair to count that wrong. Perhaps two or three degrees should be granted as leeway. Also, if *Fair* was predicted and there is a two-minute shower, do you want to mark that wrong?

Suppose the prediction was *Fair* and it turned out to be fair, even though the temperature, wind, pressure, and humidity were incorrectly predicted. How would you mark the weatherman for that?

Think about it for a while. It is probably better to

judge the man separately for each item he predicts, rather than to strike an average for all conditions.

You may end up with the conclusions that, during your testing period, the weatherman was 91 per cent cor-

DATE OF PREDIC- TION	ONE WORD PREDIC- TION	AVER- AGE TEMPER- ATURE	PRECIP- ITATION	WIND DIREC- TION	WIND SPEED M.P.H.	SKY CONDI- TION
.9-6	FAIR / CLOUDY	72. / 77	NONE / NONE	'W / SW	15 / 8	FEW CLOUDS / VERY CLOUDY ALL DAY

PREDICTION / OBSER- VATION NEXT DAY

HOW EACH RECTANGLE IS DIVIDED

rect for temperature, allowing a 2-degree difference, 76 per cent right for wind direction, and 87 per cent accurate for one-word predictions. The sample figures just given, of course, are not official.

Can cricket chirps give us the temperature?

Some biologists say that crickets chirp faster when the air is warmer. In fact, they have developed a method for discovering the temperature by listening to the ordinary cricket one finds around the house.

You are supposed to count the number of chirps in fourteen seconds and then add 40. This gives the number of degrees of temperature on the Fahrenheit scale. Check up on this. If it is not correct, can you change the formula so it is correct?

See if your corrected method is accurate by testing it on many nights, both cool and warm.

In Oriental countries crickets are kept in special small cages and selected for their song in the same way that you would select a canary in the pet shop. Try to keep a cricket in a small cage. Feed it apple cores. Do not forget to give it water, too.

Crickets do not sing as birds do. They make the sound by rubbing their wings together, as a violinist draws his bow over a string. One wing has ridges on it and the other wing is notched like a file.

The noise is made by the male only. The high notes

and low notes produced by the cricket make it hard for us to determine whether he is near us or far from us. He is the ventriloquist of the insect world.

Trial	Chirps in 14 seconds	Calculated temperature	Actual temperature measured by thermometer
1			
2			
3			
4			
5			
6			

How reliable is a milk-bottle barometer?

It is rare to see an elementary science book that does not describe the milk-bottle barometer shown in the diagram.

It demonstrates the principle of an aneroid barometer, since the pointer is supposed to rise and fall with the changes in the air pressure.

However, there is a great deal of doubt cast upon its accuracy, because even a small temperature change will expand or contract the air in the bottle. So, if it is to be used at all, it must be in a place that has an even temperature, like a home that is controlled by a thermostat.

But even under the ideal conditions, will it show variations in air pressure so that you can trust it?

Set up the barometer which is to be tested. Near it

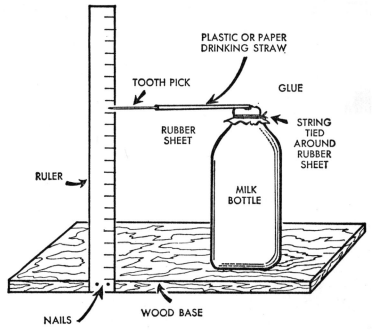

PLASTIC OR PAPER DRINKING STRAW

TOOTH PICK

GLUE

STRING TIED AROUND RUBBER SHEET

RUBBER SHEET

RULER

MILK BOTTLE

NAILS

WOOD BASE

place a thermometer and, if possible, a real aneroid barometer. If you cannot obtain this barometer, then get the correct barometric pressure from the newspaper, radio, or TV weather reports.

Keep records for a few weeks like this:

Date	Time	Milk-bottle barometer reading	Temperature	Actual barometric pressure

A study of the figures should give you the truth concerning the reliability of this homemade barometer of yours.

The ruler is not there to show actual air pressure in inches. It is used only to record up-and-down movements of the pointer.

Is the milk-bottle barometer a real scientific instrument or just something to keep around for show?

Is it warm under the snow?

Despite the inconveniences caused by a heavy snowstorm, farmers are said to like snow.

The first reason is that the ground will have water in the spring if there is sufficient melting snow.

Also, the snow acts like an insulating blanket and the warmth cannot escape from the ground beneath. The farmer has many things he wishes to protect during the winter.

Find a deep snowdrift over some earth. Record the air temperature. Lower a thermometer tied to a measuring stick at varying depths into the snow. Allow about five minutes for the thermometer to become adjusted to the new temperature.

Pull the thermometer up fast and read immediately. Make a graph plotting the degrees against the depth. Here is a sample graph. Yours will be similar but you will place your own readings on it.

Is it ever colder under the snow than it is above it?

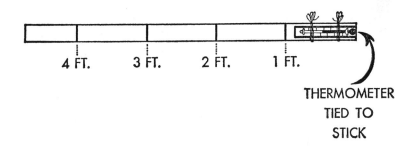

4 FT. 3 FT. 2 FT. 1 FT.

THERMOMETER
TIED TO
STICK

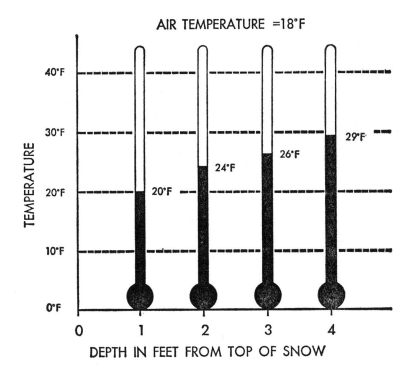

AIR TEMPERATURE =18°F

THE TEMPERATURE UNDER THE SNOW

(THIS IS ONLY A SAMPLE CHART)

More to find out:

What are the different temperatures at any moment in your neighborhood?

Chart the temperatures in the following places: in the open air, under boards and stones, in tall grass, in bushes, 2 inches under the soil, in the woods, etc. The thermometer should always be shielded from the direct sun.

Is the statement "rain before seven, clear before eleven" true?

Keep records to show how often this does and does not happen. Check other weather superstitions.

What effect does a thunderstorm have on the temperature?

Start taking the temperature very frequently before, during, and after a sudden storm. Make a graph showing time and temperature.

What is the coldest area in your refrigerator?

Test the air only. Do not allow the thermometer to touch the sides. Indicate the temperatures on a sketch of the interior of the refrigerator.

What is the temperature inside a closed automobile that is in the hot sun?

What is the effect of opening the windows 1 inch?

How much does an air-filled balloon expand when heated?

Blow up a round balloon and measure its widest circumference with a string or a tape measure. Now place it in a very warm place such as over a hot radiator or in the hot sun for a while. Measure the circumference again. Another experiment you can do is to place the balloon in the refrigerator or out in the winter air to show contraction.

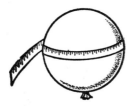

Books to read

Carroll and Mildred Fenton, *Our Changing Weather,* New York: Doubleday & Company, Inc., 1954.

Herman Schneider, *Everyday Weather and How It Works,* New York: Whittlesey House, 1951.

Ivan R. Tannehill, *Hurricane Hunters,* New York: Dodd, Mead and Company, Inc., 1956.

Herbert S. Zim, *Lightning and Thunder,* New York: William Morrow and Company, 1952.

WATER

How much water is wasted in your home?

When dry spells cause a water shortage we all become very conscious of the amount of water we waste. One of the ways we lose much water is by not repairing leaking faucets.

If you have a leaking faucet, use a measuring cup to catch the drops to see how much water is wasted in one

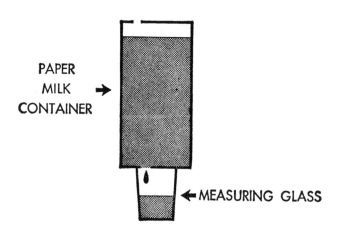

PAPER
MILK →
CONTAINER

←MEASURING GLASS

hour.   Compute how much would be wasted in a day, week, or month.

Multiply that by the number of homes in your community and you will be shocked by the total volume of these tiny drops, if every house has just one little leak.

If you wish to perform a startling demonstration for your friends, fill a large paper milk-container with water and puncture a hole in the bottom so that one drop falls per second.   Place the dripping container over a can to see how much water is lost in ten minutes.   Calculate the loss in a day.

Where else does your family waste water?

What can you do about it?

Can you control the evaporation of water?

One of the important problems for a community is collecting enough water for its citizens.   Every summer we read in the newspapers of critical water shortages in many large cities.

Engineers tell us that in addition to the careless use of water by people, tremendous quantities of good water are also lost because of the natural process of evaporation.

Recently it was found that if certain oils, especially sperm oil from whales, were spread over the water in a reservoir, more than half of the wasteful evaporation could be prevented.

You probably know that very little oil is needed to spread a thin film over water.   In this experiment you will find out how much oil you have to use to produce good results. Take four juice glasses, preferably with parallel sides. Fill each one with water to the same level, about an inch from the top. Mark the level in each glass by using a small strip of adhesive tape.

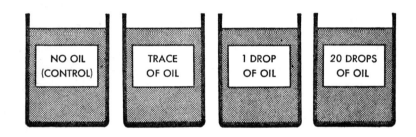

In one glass place one drop of an oil like olive oil that spreads well. Test various kinds. The film should remain over the water and not end up around the sides. Make sure the glass does not have any soap or detergent left over from the last washing because this spoils the film.

In the second glass place twenty drops of the oil you have decided to use. In the third glass merely swish an oily finger in the water. This will give it just a trace of oil.

Leave one glass without oil. This is your *control,* or basis for comparison.

Keep all glasses under the same conditions. You may hasten the evaporation by keeping all glasses on an equally warm radiator cover or in any warm spot.

Record the levels, using a ruler. Make charts and

graphs like those given here to show rates of evaporation. If you later use a different oil, make another chart.

Glass	Starting levels on March 12	New Levels				
		March 15	March 18	March 21	March 24	Total loss
No oil (control)	3″	2¾″	2⅜″	2⅛″	1⅞″	1⅛″
Trace of oil	3″					
One drop	3″					
Twenty drops	3″					

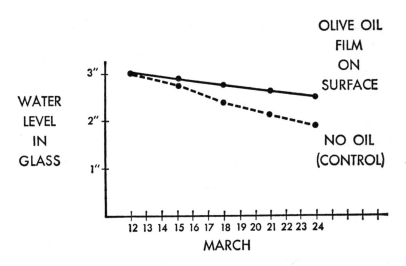

EFFECT OF OIL FILM ON
THE EVAPORATION RATE OF WATER

How much salt is there in sea water?

In some parts of the world people still evaporate water from the ocean to get table salt. See how much solid material you will get from 1 quart of water you dipped up from the ocean and evaporated.

Gently boil the water in an aluminum baking pan or a pyrex dish until only the moist salt remains. Now bake in an oven until the salt is dry.

Weigh the salt on the most sensitive scale at the grocer's or ask your druggist or anyone with a photography or chemical scale to weigh it.

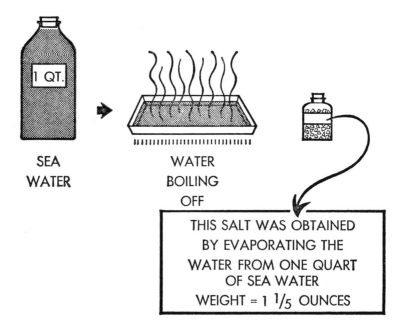

SEA
WATER

WATER
BOILING
OFF

THIS SALT WAS OBTAINED
BY EVAPORATING THE
WATER FROM ONE QUART
OF SEA WATER
WEIGHT = 1 $\frac{1}{5}$ OUNCES

If a quart of salt water gives you from 1 to 1⅓ ounces of dry salt, then you are a fairly careful worker.

The amount of dissolved salt in sea water is about 3.5–3.6 per cent.

About three-quarters of this is sodium chloride, which is commonly called table salt. Another salt is magnesium chloride. This absorbs moisture from the air in humid weather and prevents table salt (in which it is present) from pouring freely. Magnesium sulfate, commonly called Epsom salts, is also part of ocean salt. This gives sea water its slightly bitter taste. Place a tiny bit of the salt on your tongue to verify this.

Another part of dissolved sea salt is calcium bicarbonate; it is used by animals like oysters and clams for their hard shells.

Practically everything else is dissolved in sea water in very small amounts—even gold!

Is all sea water the same? Use your ingenuity to obtain sea water from distant sources. For example, the next time your neighbor takes his car to Miami or to Boston, have him bring back some ocean water.

Keep a chart showing the weight of salt obtained by evaporating the water out of 1 quart from each of your sources. You will find that there is hardly any difference for any particular latitude.

If you do not live near the sea and cannot get any ocean water, then evaporate pond or tap water. Are there many mineral salts there? Or, add about 1 ounce of table salt to a quart of water and evaporate the water as described. It is fun to see the salt come out.

More to find out:

At what temperature does the ocean freeze?

Place some sea water in a tin can. Put it in the freezer or use dry ice in a bowl to cool the container. Do not handle dry ice with your bare hands. Record the temperature at which the sea water freezes.

You can make artificial sea water for your experiment by dissolving about three tablespoonfuls of table salt in 1 quart of water. Of course, your results will not be true for sea water but you will learn that salt lowers the freezing point of water.

At what angle must you hold the garden hose so that the stream of water will go the farthest?

Can you devise a test for very fresh eggs?

All eggs have air spaces in them. The older the egg the larger the air space becomes, and therefore the egg is more buoyant in water.

A fresh egg will just about sink in fresh water. A stale egg (or even one a few days old) will float. Sometimes you may have to add a little table salt to the water so that the older egg will float. However, do not add so much salt that the fresh egg also floats. It should sink.

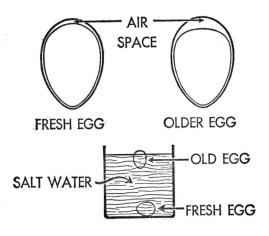

AIR SPACE

FRESH EGG   OLDER EGG

SALT WATER — OLD EGG — FRESH EGG

Does warm water weigh as much as cold water?

Use a gallon jug. Fill it with cold water and weigh it. Empty the jug, refill it with warm water, and weigh again. Be careful not to use water which is very hot because you may crack the jug.

Can boiled water get back its original taste?

Boy Scouts know that one of the best ways to get safe drinking water while camping is to boil the water to kill the germs. The water will now taste flat, mainly because the dissolved air in the water has been removed by the boiling process.

Will shaking boiled water in a not-quite-full clean jar

cause air to be dissolved in the water and give the water back its original taste? The boiled water should be cool. Taste it before and after shaking.

Does more table salt dissolve in hot water than in cold water?

Add salt to a glass of cold water until no more will dissolve no matter how well it is stirred. Keep a record of the amount that you added.

Do the same for very hot water. Be sure to use the same quantity of water as before.

Books to read

Ferdinand Cole Lane, *All About the Sea,* New York: Random House, Inc., 1953.

Raymond Faucett, *Salt,* Cambridge, Mass.: Robert Bentley, Inc., 1953.

W. M. Reed and W. S. Bronson, *The Sea for Sam,* New York: Harcourt, Brace and Company, Inc., 1935.

S. R. Riedman, *Water for People,* New York: Henry Schuman, Inc., Publishers, 1952.

INSECTS

Can you read by firefly light?

Fireflies are easy to catch. Some night when they are plentiful, fill a glass jar with as many as you can. Is it true that you can read a newspaper by their light?

Some folks call them glowworms, but they are really beetles. The tip of the abdomen flashes a light on and off. The female has no wings and is therefore near or on the ground. She has a much stronger light than the flying male. You can see her flashes in the grass. Some scientists believe that by shining her light on and off in a certain rhythm she can attract the male down to her.

Try shining your flashlight underneath the jar of fireflies at different intervals from one to four seconds apart. If you do not have a jar of them, shine the flashlight near the grass when the fireflies are overhead. See if you can make them light up in answer to your flashings. It can be done, but they will respond best only at a certain flashing rate between one and four seconds.

Put a thermometer into the jar of fireflies. Does the light from the fireflies make the temperature rise? Place a thermometer in a similar empty jar as a control.

Nobody knows exactly what causes the light produced

by fireflies. Read about cold light in an encyclopedia. This is the kind of light a firefly produces.

How far can an insect jump?

Have you ever been fascinated by the science-fiction stories about how strong insects are and how far they can jump for their size and weight? Here are suggestions for finding out for yourself the amazing truth about this.

When you go into the fields with your ruler and notebook you will find many kinds of hopping insects. Some will use wings and combine some flying with each hop. Disregard these.

Measure the insect you decide to use very carefully with a ruler having markings for every sixteenth or thirty-second of an inch. Measure from the tip of the head to the tip of the abdomen. Then place the wingless grasshopper, cricket, or whatever you decide to use on unobstructed ground that will enable you to measure jumps and to recover the insect. Get the average of twenty jumps.

Suppose you find that a 1-inch grasshopper jumped 50 inches. That means that it jumped fifty times its own length. Now, if you could do that, and you were 5 feet tall, you could jump 250 feet!

If you want to astonish yourself with a most unbelievable bit of information, try this next research. Find out how far a man could jump if he had the ability of an insect—but this time use weight instead of size as the basis for comparison.

Ask your druggist to weigh a jumping insect. If you are using a tiny insect, and it is impossible to get an accurate reading, then you can weigh many of them at the same time. By dividing the total weight by the number of insects, the approximate weight of one is obtained.

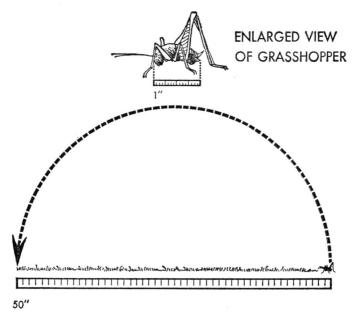

ENLARGED VIEW OF GRASSHOPPER

1"

50"

Let us say that your insect weighed one-hundredth of an ounce (0.01 oz.) and could jump 3 feet. Now change your own weight into ounces. There are 16 ounces in a pound—remember? If you weigh 100 pounds, you weigh 100×16 or 1,600 ounces. To find out how many times 0.01 ounce your 1,600 ounces are, make a fraction $\dfrac{1,600}{0.01}$. Reducing this fraction gives you the information that you are 160,000 times as heavy as the insect. So, if you could jump as well as it can for its weight, you could jump 160,000 times as far as 3 feet, or 480,000 feet. Change that to miles by dividing by 5,280 since there are that many feet in a mile.

You will arrive at the utterly fantastic conclusion that you would be able to leap about 91 miles!

But work out your own research and see what results you get. It should be lots of fun. Remember, of course, that comparing a man with an insect this way may be interesting but it is scientifically wrong!

Here is a teaser to work out by direct observation. Find out whether a 2-inch grasshopper jumps twice as far as a 1-inch grasshopper.

Look at the legs of a grasshopper under a magnifying glass and maybe you will see why this insect is such a good jumper.

Where are the ants going?

If you want scientific activity that will keep you out in the fresh air, study the behavior of some busy ants.

Follow the motion of an ant for fifteen minutes. Where is it going? Does it travel in a straight path? Does it travel for a considerable distance? Pick it up carefully with a stiff piece of paper and place it where it was a short time before. Does it go back in the general direction that it took before?

Does it move at the same speed all the time? What is it bringing to the anthill? You can identify your ant

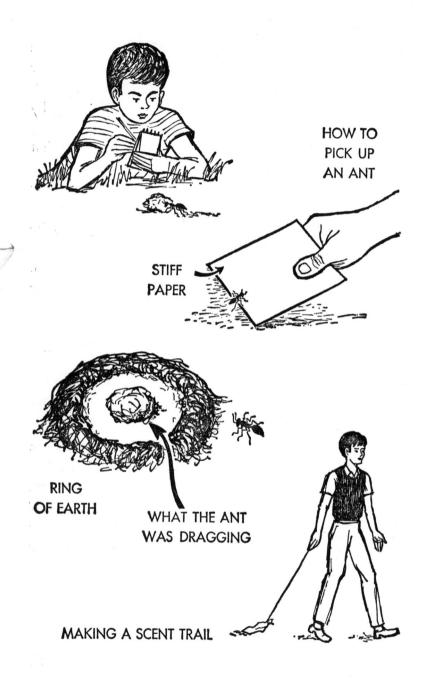

HOW TO
PICK UP
AN ANT

STIFF
PAPER

RING
OF EARTH

WHAT THE ANT
WAS DRAGGING

MAKING A SCENT TRAIL

in a crowd by placing a tiny dot of brightly colored fast-drying airplane dope or red nail polish on the back of its thigh.

How much greater than its own size is the material that it is dragging? If you take away from an ant something that it is struggling with, will it recover the substance and continue its journey?

Try placing a ring of earth, wire, benzene, or cologne around the substance. Will the ant cross the obstruction to recover the load, or will it lose all interest?

Put a piece of food near an anthill. See how many ants finally come out to pull it in. Now put down another piece two times the size of the first. Will twice as many ants arrive to pull it?

Make a scent trial by dragging a cloth soaked in molasses along the ground, starting at the anthill. Will ants move along this trail? Try different scents.

Famous naturalists have discovered many interesting facts from watching ants in this same way. Ask your librarian for books that these people have written.

How fast do some insects and small animals move?

How fast do insects move over the ground? How does the speed of an ant compare with that of a beetle, caterpillar, or centipede? With another small animal such as a snail, worm, or turtle?

There are many interesting experiments that you can perform by building a miniature "measured mile."

Make a shallow groove in the earth about 1 foot long. Time each creature as it moves from the starting point to the finish line.

If the insect or whatever you use decides to wander, a little touch will steer it back along the straight path. Test each one a few times to get the average speed.

What makes them go faster? Loud noises, sun, shade, perfume, or the smell at the finish line of the food they usually eat?

To find out whether cooling an insect makes it go more sluggishly, first clock it a few times to get its accurate speed. Then place it in the refrigerator so it cools off. Record the temperature and length of time it was cooled. Now time it on the track. What happened to its speed? Does it show any other unusual behavior?

Do insects go up a tree trunk at the same speed that they go down?

Make a chart in your research notebook showing the speeds of the animals in your "racing stable."

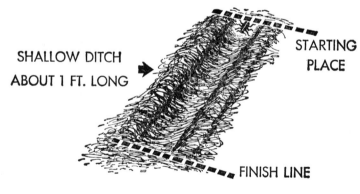

SHALLOW DITCH
ABOUT 1 FT. LONG

STARTING
PLACE

FINISH LINE

MINIATURE RACE TRACK

Animal	Number of seconds to move 1 foot	Miles per day
Small ant		
Large ant		
Beetle		
Caterpillar		
Centipede		
Snail		
Worm		
Turtle		

To calculate the miles per day, follow this reasoning:

If it moves ⎯ 1 foot in 30 seconds
then it moves 2 feet in ⎯ 1 minute
or 120 feet in ⎯ 1 hour.

120×24 hours $= 2,880$ feet per day

$\dfrac{2,880}{5,280} =$ about ½ mile per day

More to find out:

What will a caterpillar become?

Place the caterpillar in a jar with some leaves of the plant on which it was feeding when found. Sprinkle

water on the leaves. Cover the jar with something which allows air to pass. Watch the insect spin a cocoon or form a chrysalis. A moth or butterfly will emerge.

How can you study ants?

A simple home for ants is an open-topped glass jar, placed in a pan of water to prevent their escape. Put earth into the jar and also many different-looking ants from the same anthill. Place an inverted carton over the entire pan. When viewing, lift the carton.

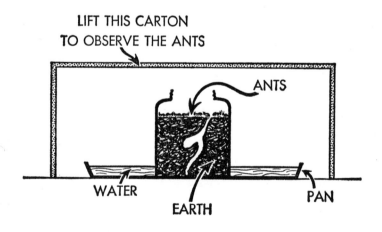

LIFT THIS CARTON
TO OBSERVE THE ANTS

ANTS

WATER

EARTH

PAN

What colored lights attract moths and other insects at night?

Use a yellow, white, blue, or red electric bulb, or one of another color. Make sure that the wattages are the same and that the lights are about 3 feet apart. Most people find that blue bulbs attract insects while yellow bulbs are actually used to repel them.

How does a praying mantis eat?

Next time you get a praying mantis, place it in a jar with a cover that has holes for air to enter. Feed it different live insects and record how it uses the spines on its front limbs to hold the victim. Do not forget water.

What cocoons are these?

Wintertime is a good time to collect many kinds of cocoons. Place each one in a jar but do not keep them too warm or they will emerge before spring. Sprinkle them with water once in a while. See what emerges. Leave a long twig in each jar so the moth can dry its wings smoothly.

How can you make a beetle trap?

Bury a long empty olive jar or tin can so that the top is flush with the ground. Place some meat in the trap. The beetle cannot escape once it falls in.

Are bees attracted to certain colors?

Place some honey on a piece of red paper. Dab the same amount on a piece of paper of the same size but another color.　See if bees are attracted more to certain colors.

How can fruit flies be raised for experiments?

Keep an overripe banana or a decaying piece of apple in an open jar outside.　Tiny fruit flies will be attracted. Capture a few and cover the jar.　Make holes for air.　In a few weeks you will have hundreds.

How many young are there in a praying mantis egg mass?

Books to read

C. L. Fenton and D. C. Pallas, *Insects and Their World,* New York: The John Day Company, Inc., 1956.

W. J. Holland, *The Butterfly Book,* New York: Doubleday & Company, Inc.

Lois J. Hussey and Catherine Pessino, *Collecting Cocoons,* New York: Thomas Crowell Company, 1953.

Ferdinand Lane, *All About the Insect World,* New York: Random House, Inc., 1954.

Paul M. Sears, *Firefly,* New York: Holiday House, Inc., 1956.

Ralph B. Swain, *The Insect Guide,* New York: Doubleday & Company, Inc., 1948.

Edwin Way Teale, *The Junior Book of Insects,* New York: E. P. Dutton & Co., Inc., 1953.

How much water is in an apple?

The apple you bit into today certainly was juicy, wasn't it? It should be interesting to know how much water there really is in an apple.

When you do this experiment, run a few tests at the same time.

First, weigh the apple. Then, in order to hasten the evaporation of water, slice, chop, or grate the apple. Finally, when drying is complete, weigh the pieces. The loss of weight is the amount of water that was in the apple.

Keep the pieces in an aluminum pie plate. Place in a warm spot, such as over a hot radiator or in a sunny window. Do not place in a baking oven. Try not to lose a single piece.

It is best to use a delicate photography or chemical scale, or ask your friendly druggist to do the weighing for you. The sensitive scale used by your grocer or butcher may also be used.

Get the weight of the pie plate first. Then subtract that amount from the total weight of the plate and the

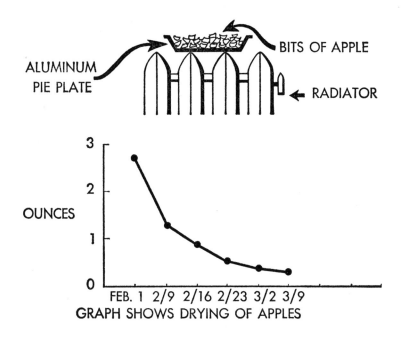

ALUMINUM PIE PLATE

BITS OF APPLE

RADIATOR

OUNCES

FEB. 1 2/9 2/16 2/23 3/2 3/9

GRAPH SHOWS DRYING OF APPLES

pieces of apple. The difference is the weight of the apple.

How long must the pieces dry? In a few days the bits of apple are going to become as hard as pebbles, and they will bounce about on the plate. They will shrink in a most surprising manner and turn a brown color.

Allow a long time for drying. The time to end the tests is when the pieces do not lose any more weight. This may take a few weeks. Keep records of each weighing. Make a graph showing the rate of drying of your apples.

The form which follows may be useful:

	Test 1	Date
Weight of apple at start	2.7 oz.	Feb. 1
Weight of dried apple	0.3 oz.	March 9
Weight of water in apple	2.4 oz.	

The weight of the water, as you can see, is obtained by subtracting line 2 from line 1.

Make a large chart using the items in the above form. Include spaces for several additional tests and their dates.

Calculate your results this way:

$$\frac{\text{Weight of water in apple}}{\text{Weight of apple at start}} \times 100 = \text{Percentage of water in apple.}$$

For your final result, get the average of all your tests.

Does it help to start flowering bulbs in the dark?

Narcissus, hyacinth, and daffodil bulbs, when planted indoors, are usually kept in the dark for several weeks.

There are two reasons for this: to develop a good root system so that the flowering plant will be healthier, and to delay blooming while this growth is taking place.

Many people are not convinced about the value of this waiting period, especially if they want flowers in a hurry.

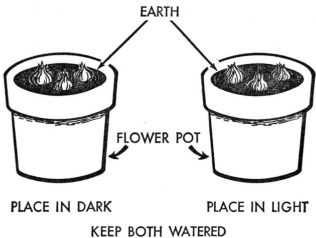

EARTH

FLOWER POT

PLACE IN DARK   PLACE IN LIGHT

KEEP BOTH WATERED

In your experiment, you can learn if this waiting period makes a big enough difference in the size and number of flowers, the duration of blooming, and the general condition of the plant.

Obtain six similar bulbs and set up three in the dark and three in the light. Use a pot of soil for each group of three, or just water and pebbles in a bowl. Use the same conditions for each pot except for the light. All

BULBS MAY ALSO BE PLANTED
IN PEBBLES AND WATER

the bulbs should be kept moist and well ventilated. Let one pot remain in the dark and the other in the light until many roots come out. Then place the bulbs which were in the dark in the light next to the others.

The bulbs in the light will bloom first, so take careful notes concerning the flowers and leaves.

Compare with the bulbs that were in the dark.

Copy this chart in your research notebook and fill in your observations.

	Kept in dark			Kept in light		
Bulb No.	1	2	3	4	5	6
Planting date						
Date bulbs were placed in sunlight						
Blooming date						
Size of leaves						
Number of leaves						
Number of blossoms						
Height of plant						
General condition of plant						
Number of days in good bloom						

Do all vines twine in the same direction?

There is a belief among many gardeners that all vines in the Northern Hemisphere wind themselves around a string or a twig in the same direction. Their theory is that this tendency is caused by the rotation of the earth.

Why not learn more about this subject by looking around and keeping notes on your observations?

Morning glories, some ivy plants, peas, beans, and honeysuckle are just a few plants to observe.

Record your directions as *clockwise* or *counterclock-*

DIRECTION THAT THE VINE IS TWINING WHEN
VIEWED FROM ABOVE

CLOCKWISE   COUNTER-
                 CLOCKWISE

THIS VINE IS GROWING
AROUND THE POST IN A
COUNTERCLOCKWISE
DIRECTION VIEWED
FROM ABOVE

wise as viewed from above: *Clockwise* means turning like the hands of a clock.

Do all plants of the same kind wind around something in the same direction? If not, do they seem to favor one direction over the other?

Fill in the chart for other plants. Make many observations of a certain kind of plant.

How would you find out how long it takes for a vine to make one complete loop?

One of the explanations of twining is that the part of the vine that touches the string or twig does not grow as fast as the other cells. This produces the curling. Of course, this does not explain why the vine twines in one direction.

Plant	Make a check mark (√) for each observation	
	Clockwise	Counterclockwise
Morning glory		
English ivy		
Boston ivy		
Wisteria		
Honeysuckle		
Peas		
Beans		
Other twining plants		

How fast do some plants grow?

How much does a vine grow in one day?

What part of a plant grows fastest?

Do plants grow faster in the springtime than in mid-summer?

Do plants grow faster during rainy spells?

These and many more stimulating questions can be answered if you experiment with a long vine such as honeysuckle.

Indicate the starting place for your careful measurements by tying one or two loops of string on the vine about an inch or so from the tip, as shown in the illustration. Do not squeeze, cut, or otherwise injure the plant. If you have waterproof ink you may use that to mark the vine.

Make a trial test first to see how fast the end of the vine grows. This will give you an idea of how often to take measurements. Perhaps once a week may be sufficient.

At the end of your experiment divide the total increase in length by the number of days. Your answer will be the average growth per day.

To find out which part of the vine grows, tie two markers of string exactly 12 inches apart, near the bottom of the vine. Do the same in the middle of the vine and also near the end (do not include the tip). Take careful measurements at weekly intervals for a month.

You will be surprised to learn that a plant grows in length mainly from the tip-end of the stem.

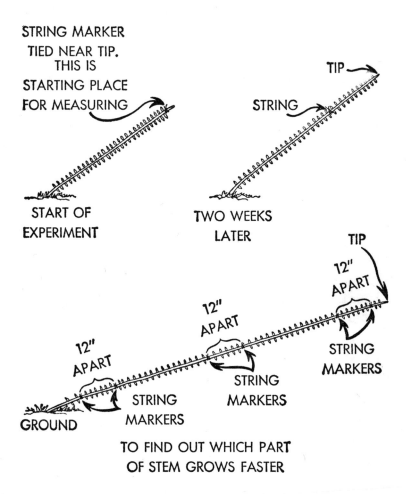

STRING MARKER TIED NEAR TIP. THIS IS STARTING PLACE FOR MEASURING

START OF EXPERIMENT

TIP

STRING

TWO WEEKS LATER

TIP

12" APART

12" APART

12" APART

STRING MARKERS

STRING MARKERS

STRING MARKERS

GROUND

TO FIND OUT WHICH PART OF STEM GROWS FASTER

You may want to use charts like those on the next page.

Date of measurement	Kind of weather between measurements	Distance from end of vine to marker
Start $7/10$	$7/10$ clear	$1\frac{5}{16}''$
	$7/11$ clear	
	$7/12$ rain	
	$7/13$ rain	
	$7/14$ cloudy	
$7/15$	$7/15$ clear	$2\frac{3}{16}''$

Where the vine was marked 12" apart	Starting date	Ending date	Distance between markers at end of experiment
4" from ground	$7/21$		
2' from ground	$7/21$		
6' from ground and 2" from tip	$7/21$		

More to find out:

How does a tree grow?

Hammer two nails exactly 3 feet apart in the trunk of a young tree. (Secure permission first!) See if they ever grow apart even though we know that branches grow in length at their tips.

How much weight can soaked beans lift as they expand?

Fill a small jar or tin can with beans. Add water and cover with a flat piece of wood or metal. Place heavy weights on top.

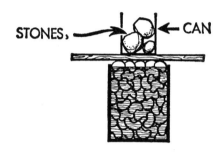

STONES, ← CAN

Do green plants produce oxygen faster in stronger sunlight?

Place a sprig of a water plant such as elodea in a quart jar filled with water. Keep it in strong sunlight. When

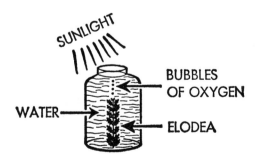

SUNLIGHT

BUBBLES OF OXYGEN

WATER

ELODEA

the bubbles of oxygen come up from the plant count the number per minute. Do it many times to get a true figure. Now shade the jar and count the bubbles again. Do it in the early morning sun too. You can see what effect cold has on the rate in the wintertime by placing the jar outside the window but still in the sun.

How many seeds will sprout?

Place as many seeds as you can about 1 inch apart on a moist towel and roll it up. Keep the towel moist. Examine from time to time. Calculate your results this way:

$$\frac{\text{Number of seeds that sprouted}}{\text{Number of seeds used}} \times 100 = \text{Percentage that sprouted.}$$

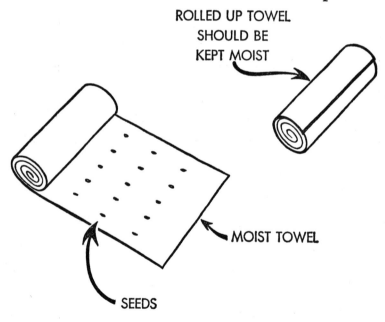

ROLLED UP TOWEL
SHOULD BE
KEPT MOIST

MOIST TOWEL

SEEDS

The seed packet calls this percentage *viability* or *germination* and gives a figure. See if you agree with that number.

How long does it take for some leaves to turn toward the sun?

Start off with a plant like a geranium, whose leaves are all facing in one direction. Does it take longer to turn the leaves of a plant that has not been turned for a very long time?

Can you make a map showing the different trees in your neighborhood?

If you do not know the name of each tree, use a book describing trees or ask the owner.

Books to read

Richard R. Kinney, *Guide to Gardening with Young People,* Englewood Cliffs, N.J.: Prentice-Hall, Inc., 1955.

Herbert McKay, *Easy Experiments with Plants,* New York: Oxford University Press, 1931.

Herman Schneider, *Plants in the City,* The John Day Company, Inc., 1951.

Herbert S. Zim, *What's Inside of Plants,* New York: William Morrow and Company, 1952.

DISTANCE

How far away is the North Pole?

This problem looks simple, yet if thirty students worked on it, there would be thirty different answers.

The reason is that there are many types of maps. Most of them are out of proportion near the North and South Poles. You will not get true distances if you lay a ruler on a map and measure the distance from your home town to the pole, even if you use the scale shown at the bottom of the map.

Look at many maps. Estimate the distance on each. Ask your friends to do the same.

When estimating distances on a map, remember that the shortest distance going directly north is on a meridian.

And since you are using airplane distances, perhaps a well-written letter to the right people at an airport will give you a verified check on your findings.

In this exercise we are referring to the geographic North Pole and not the magnetic North Pole to which the compass needle points. These are two different places, you know.

Put a large arrow in your room pointing to the North Pole. Print the miles on it.

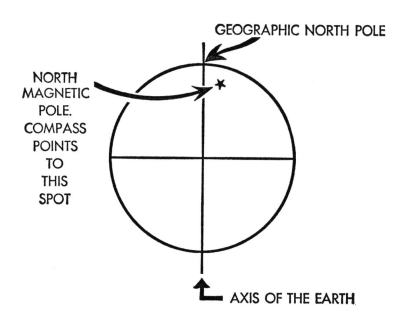

GEOGRAPHIC NORTH POLE

NORTH
MAGNETIC
POLE.
COMPASS
POINTS
TO
THIS
SPOT

AXIS OF THE EARTH

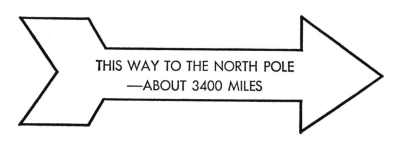

THIS WAY TO THE NORTH POLE
—ABOUT 3400 MILES

DISTANCE FROM PINEVILLE
TO THE NORTH POLE

	Miles
My estimate	3,400
Average class estimate	3,215
La Guardia Airport figures	3,327
Uncle Joe (Lt. in Air Force)	3,320
Civil Engineer at City Hall	3,316
Mr. Dan of the Planetarium	3,331
Almanac	3,327

How high above sea level are you?

Do you have a clear idea of how high above sea level you are at this moment?

There is an easy way to find out. All through your neighborhood there are certain reference points used all the time by surveyors and civil engineers. These are called *bench marks* or *monuments.*

They are small concrete or bronze blocks, perhaps with little crosses cut into them. You must have passed them many times. You just did not know what they were. They are usually found imbedded in the sidewalks near corners, or on statues in parks, or on steps in public buildings.

In New York City the metal plate which covers each bench mark is inscribed MONUMENT OF BUREAU OF TOPOGRAPHY. In other cities there may be other identification.

The easiest way to find these reference points is to phone the proper department in your town or city and

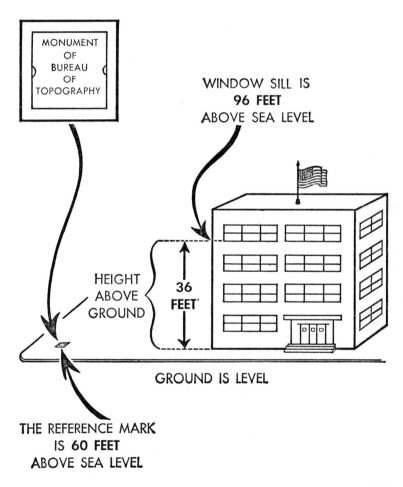

MONUMENT
OF
BUREAU
OF
TOPOGRAPHY

WINDOW SILL IS
96 FEET
ABOVE SEA LEVEL

HEIGHT
ABOVE
GROUND

**36
FEET**

GROUND IS LEVEL

THE REFERENCE MARK
IS **60 FEET**
ABOVE SEA LEVEL

tell them what you want. The City Surveyors, Department of Public Works, Bureau of Topography, Real Estate Division, Bureau of Sewers, and Engineering Department all use these markers. Your town should have one of these offices.

Ask them for the closest bench mark to your school. They will tell you exactly where it is and also the elevation above sea level.

Now, if the ground is level, then anything on the ground in the neighborhood will have the same elevation as the marker.

If the ground slopes you may estimate how much higher or lower the bottom of the school is than the marker.

Find out the height of your science room from the ground. You can now determine the elevation of the teacher's desk. (See the illustration.)

Get the rest of the class to share in the expense of a small professionally engraved metal plate which will be forever fastened to her desk. Each student will have to donate only a dime. Your teacher will remember your class until the day she retires.

The brass plate may state:

THE ELEVATION OF THIS DESK
IS 95 FEET ABOVE SEA LEVEL.
DETERMINED BY CLASS 6^3,
APRIL, 1959.

Find the elevation of a few places in your neighborhood or town. Include the desk in your own room at home. Make a chart listing these places and their elevations above sea level.

How high is the auditorium ceiling?

What would you do to find the answer to this puzzler? Think about it.

Is there a ladder big enough? What does the custodian do when he has to change a bulb? Maybe that is a clue.

How about tying together many big sticks or bamboo poles and reaching the ceiling with them?

Perhaps if you knew the size of the stage curtains you might do some careful estimating of the rest of the distances.

Try standing in the rear of the auditorium and have a friend whose height you know stand in the front. Then compare his height with the height of the ceiling. Can you get the answer this way? (See the illustration on page 114.)

If there is a balcony, can you see how the problem becomes simpler?

There must be dozens of good ideas to try. Ask your friends.

A very simple method is given on the next page. Can you find an easier way?

Go to a toy store or any other store that can fill a balloon with helium gas. Many high-school chemistry

5 FEET

5 FEET

5 FEET

5 FEET

5 FEET

departments have small cylinders of this gas. Weathermen at airports also have tanks.

Attach a string to the balloon and allow it to rise to the ceiling. Get the vertical distance. Beware of drafts. Measure the string and do not forget to include the height of the balloon itself.

And when you are all through, ask the custodian to look at the school blueprints he keeps in his files. Compare your answer with the information given in the blueprints.

How high is your school?

There are many fascinating ways of finding the height of a building. Try your hand at some methods dreamed up by you or suggested by your friends.

Here is one you might use to verify your other schemes. It is based on the general idea that tall objects cast longer shadows than short objects. In this case the building casts the long shadow and a 3-foot ruler is going to be the short object.

See the shadow made by the building on a sunny day. Now get the length of the shadow of a vertical yardstick. Mark off this length on a piece of wood, paper, or string. See how many times this distance goes into the shadow of the building.

Multiply the number of times by three and the answer is the height of the building in feet.

For example, if the shadow of the yardstick goes into the shadow of the building twenty times, then the building is 60 feet high.

Now check by asking the custodian how close you came to the correct figure.

You can find the height of trees, poles, cliffs, and other high places in the same way. You can also calculate the height of a kite by standing directly underneath it and measuring the distance to its shadow.

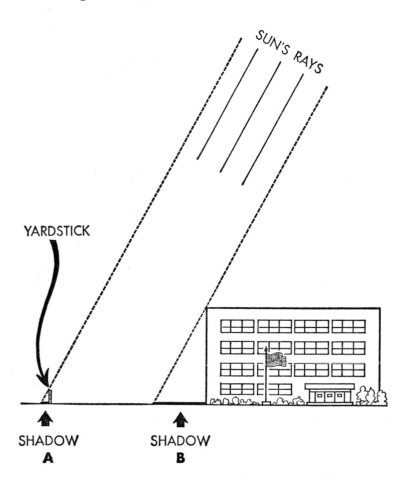

YARDSTICK

SUN'S RAYS

SHADOW
A

SHADOW
B

More to find out:

How accurately does your father's car record the miles?

In the speedometer dial there is a recorder for miles, called an *odometer*. How does it compare in accuracy with those in other cars? Is there a measured distance in your neighborhood? Does the air pressure in the tires make a difference that you can measure? Have your father drive for 1 mile and mark the starting and finishing line. Then do it again with the tires overinflated or underinflated. At what tire pressure does the odometer read correctly?

How big is a crater on the moon?

Get a large photograph of the moon. Pick out a crater you are interested in. Carefully measure with a ruler the diameter of the crater and also the diameter of the moon. Use a ruler divided into sixteenths of an inch. The actual diameter of the moon is 2,160 miles. Follow this guide:

$$\text{Approximate diameter of crater in miles} = \frac{\text{Diameter of crater in picture}}{\text{Diameter of moon in picture}} \times 2{,}160.$$

How far away is the lightning?

Lightning is seen almost instantaneously. The thunder it produces travels at approximately ⅕ mile per second. As soon as you see a flash, start counting seconds until you hear the thunder. Multiply the number of seconds by ⅕ to learn the number of miles away the lightning struck.

How thick is a newspaper page?

Lay pieces of newspaper on top of each other until you have a pile at least 1 inch high. Squeeze the paper to remove the wrinkles and trapped air. The thickness of one sheet is equal to the height divided by the number of layers. Do it many times and get an average. Write your daily newspaper for verification.

Books to read

Nelson Beeler and Franklyn Branley, *Experiments with Airplane Instruments,* New York: Thomas Y. Crowell Company, 1953.

Jeanne Bendick, *How Much and How Many,* New York: Whittlesey House, 1947.

Lancelot Hogben, *The Wonderful World of Mathematics,* New York: Garden City Books, 1955.

Trevor Lloyd, *Sky Highways,* Boston: Houghton Mifflin Company, 1945.

Beulah Tannenbaum and Myra Stillman, *Understanding Maps,* New York: Whittlesey House, 1957.

TIME

Can you split seconds accurately?

A very exact way to count seconds without a timepiece is to make a pendulum from a piece of string with a small weight tied to the end. The total length of the pendulum should be 39 inches. Swing the weight and you will discover that each swing, from one side to the other side, takes exactly one second. You should get exactly 60 swings in one minute. If the pendulum is slow, make the string a tiny bit shorter. If the pendulum is fast, lengthen the string. Every eighth of an inch makes a difference.

Do not worry about the weight on the bottom or the width of the swing. The only thing that can change the time of each swing is the length of the pendulum. A little research on your part will convince you of this. Try heavier and lighter weights. Time big and small swings with a clock or a watch having a second hand, and see that they take the same time.

If you shorten the length of the string you can get half-second swings, or even faster ones. To get better accuracy with faster swings, count the number of swings in thirty seconds. Then divide thirty seconds by the

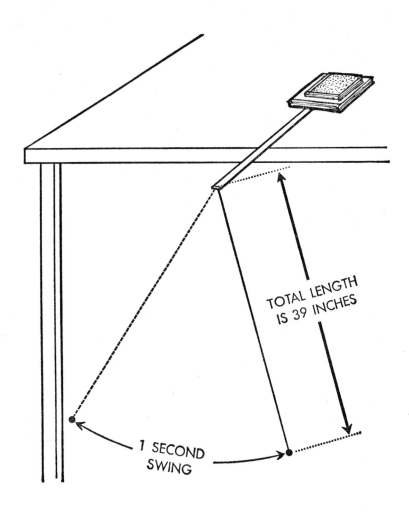

TOTAL LENGTH IS 39 INCHES

1 SECOND SWING

number of swings to find the time for one swing. For example, if you count 120 swings in thirty seconds, then one swing is equal to $\frac{30}{120}$ or one-fourth of a second for each swing.

This device can be used with very good results to time an echo for the purpose of measuring distances. Sound, as you know, travels about 1,100 feet per second. Release a pendulum which has a swing of one-fifth of a second, just as you make a loud noise.

Start counting swings. Stop when you hear the echo. Suppose you counted eleven swings. That means that the sound traveled for $1\frac{1}{5}$ seconds or $2\frac{1}{5}$ seconds. At 1,100 feet per second, we calculate that the sound traveled 2,420 feet. But the wall or cliff is half that distance away, or 1,210 feet.

A pendulum timer can also be helpful in darkroom work in photography.

Can your clock be too hot or too cold?

The hairspring in a clock or watch is the thin coiled wire you can see moving like a coiled pendulum. The shorter it is, the faster it goes. Its motion regulates a timepiece.

Do you think that putting a clock in a refrigerator, a deep-freeze cabinet, or a very cold place in the wintertime would contract the metal of the hairspring and make the clock go too fast?

Let us test this theory, but first you must protect your timepiece from moisture by placing it in a plastic bag that is free from holes and tying the end of the bag closed. You can also use a jar with a cover that has a watertight washer. Use an old clock for this experiment.

Start each test by setting the clock the same as an

electric clock or a watch that you are sure is keeping good time.

The time interval for your tests should be about twenty-four hours, or any long interval, but keep this time the same for all tests.

First do the tests at room temperatures to see how your clock behaves normally. To test a clock in a very warm spot you can place it in a covered coffee can and keep it in the hot sun in the summertime. Keep it over a hot steam radiator in the winter.

Do each test a few times to make sure. Do not spoil the clock by using very high temperatures. If possible, record the temperature.

HAIRSPRING

CLOCK IS INSIDE
COFFEE CAN

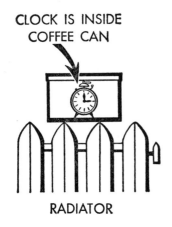

RADIATOR

TIE IN PLASTIC BAG
BEFORE PUTTING
INTO REFRIGERATOR

		Time begun	Time ended	Minutes gained or lost in 24 hours
Cold spot	Test 1			
	Test 2			
	Test 3			
Room temperature	Test 1			
	Test 2			
	Test 3			
Warm spot	Test 1			
	Test 2			
	Test 3			

Find out from a jeweller or from an encyclopedia how expensive watches and clocks are automatically adjusted for temperature changes.

How fast are you walking?

Do you know your average walking speed? If you do, you can find out how far away some place is just by seeing how long it takes you to get there. On the other hand, if you know the distance of your destination, you are able to tell exactly how long it is going to take you to walk there.

People who have this ability are seldom in a hurry because they know how much time to allow to walk somewhere.

How does one go about developing this knowledge? Well, if you walked for one hour and knew exactly how far you walked, then you would know your speed per hour.

But we can get the same result by seeing how many seconds it takes to walk only one-tenth of a mile.

The easiest way to lay out one-tenth of a mile is to have someone measure this short distance with his automobile. On the speedometer there is a numbered wheel which records tenths of miles.

Another way is to measure 528 feet, a tenth of a mile, by using the length of your stride or by counting similar sidewalk boxes.

Of course, a tape measure would be perfect, but, whichever method you use, make sure you are accurate. Check by repeating the measuring or by using different methods and comparing results.

Always start walking when the second hand of your watch is at 60 because you will be able to remember your starting place more easily. Walk at an even pace. Count the total time in seconds and look at the chart to get your speed.

STARTING LINE

END OF 1/10 OF A MILE

Seconds to walk $\frac{1}{10}$ mile	Speed in miles per hour	Seconds to walk $\frac{1}{10}$ mile	Speed in miles per hour
180	2.0	97	3.7
171	2.1	95	3.8
164	2.2	92	3.9
157	2.3	90	4.0
150	2.4	88	4.1
144	2.5	86	4.2
138	2.6	84	4.3
133	2.7	82	4.4
129	2.8	80	4.5
124	2.9	78	4.6
120	3.0	77	4.7
116	3.1	75	4.8
113	3.2	74	4.9
109	3.3	72	5.0
106	3.4	71	5.1
103	3.5	69	5.2
100	3.6	68	5.3

After a few trials you will be able to judge your speed fairly accurately. Clock the rate of a long-legged fast walker, and also the speed of your little brother or sister.

If you wish to get the speed in miles per hour of a running animal, or a sprinting friend, or someone on a bicycle, divide 360 by the number of seconds it takes to cover one-tenth of a mile.

More to find out:

Does warm water drip faster than cold water?

Many years ago, before spring clocks were invented, the hours used to be measured by the dripping of water from a water clock called a clepsydra. Do the following to show whether the clepsydra will keep wrong time if the temperature of the water changes.

Make a very small hole in a tin can so that the water falls in fast drops. Fill up to the brim and record the time it takes for the can to be emptied. Try this experiment with water of different temperatures.

What can a shadow stick tell us?

Stand a vertical stick in a sunny place. At exactly noon, one or two days a week, measure the length of the shadow. The shorter the shadow, the higher is the sun. Keep records for a few months. Make bar graphs and see how the sun's height differs through the seasons.

When do the days get longer?

By consulting calendars and almanacs make a chart to show that even though the days start getting longer after December 21, the sun does not rise earlier. It takes almost a month before that occurs. Instead, the sun sets later.

At what point does the sun rise?

Stand in the same spot and use TV aerials, chimneys, or spaces between buildings as markers. Observe and record where the sun sets. Do this whenever you think of it over a period of a year, but especially on March 21, June 21, September 23, and December 21. By this means the ancient people used to know when the seasons began.

Will a candle burn twice as long in an inverted quart jar as it will in a pint jar?

Books to read

Irving Adler, *Time in Your Life*, New York: The John Day Company, Inc., 1955.

K. Britton, *What Makes It Tick?* Boston: Houghton Mifflin Company, 1943.

Tannenbaum, Beulah and Stillman, Myra, *Understanding Time*, New York: Whittlesey House, 1958.

SCIENCE IN
YOUR HOME

How safe is your can opener?

Most modern can openers cause fine particles of metal to fall into the food. Some even drop dangerous spirals of metal into the can which is being opened.

How can you be sure that yours is not guilty?

Obtain a few empty cans of different sizes and wash them thoroughly with soap and hot water. Do the same with the can opener.

Place a clean, dry can, with the open end down, on a piece of clear, unprinted, glossy paper. Now use the dry can opener to remove the top. Tap the can and the cutout top to cause adhering particles to drop.

Keep away from drafts. Even talking or breathing hard may blow the fine dust away.

To prove that these particles are mainly iron, move a magnet *under* the paper and watch for movement above. Use a magnifying glass to see how sharp the slivers are.

Try cans of various diameters. Some openers are safe on wide cans but are defective with smaller ones.

Make sure that the particles are not coming from the outside of the can, where the notched driving wheel digs

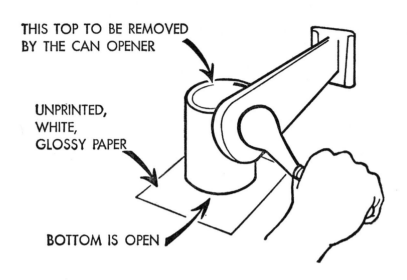

THIS TOP TO BE REMOVED
BY THE CAN OPENER

UNPRINTED,
WHITE,
GLOSSY PAPER

BOTTOM IS OPEN

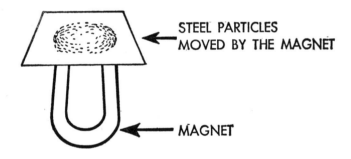

STEEL PARTICLES
MOVED BY THE MAGNET

MAGNET

into the bottom of the rim. These particles do not fall
into the food.

Of course, a tin can is really made of iron which is
coated with a small amount of tin. The tin prevents the
iron from rusting and spoiling the food. Sometimes the
inside of the can is coated with lacquer.

How effective is a magnetic-type can opener which holds the top of the can after it is cut off? Look carefully to see if it prevents particles from falling.

If the can opener is defective, you can buy new cutting blades for a few cents from the manufacturer. But that does not always solve the problem. You may have to buy a new opener.

Examine the can opener carefully. What actually causes the particles and slivers to form? Perhaps a tiny adjustment may remedy the difficulty.

Can you remove chewing gum by freezing?

Sooner or later you are going to step or sit on chewing gum. Now is the time to learn what to do when the problem arises.

The stickiness of chewing gum is lost when it is frozen stiff. Can you use this fact to remove it from substances such as woven cloth, leather, metal, wood, paper, or linoleum?

The theory sounds too simple. What are some of the problems you may encounter? Try it and see. Also, be warned that when delicate cloth is frozen stiff, rough handling may ruin it.

Prepare each sample with a sticky mess of gum. Use the freezer to harden the gum.

If the gum is still not solid enough, try using dry ice. You can obtain this from your ice-cream dealer. Remember that dry ice is very dangerous and must be handled with tongs or heavy gloves. Do not keep any in your bare hands for more than one or two seconds.

Will dry ice remove gooey gum from linoleum or from wooden floors and chairs?

If your research fails to remove all the gum, benzine or other cleaning fluids may do the job.

Can you cool drinking water with a wet towel?

You feel refreshed when you wash yourself mainly because of the cooling effect of evaporation. It takes heat to change the slight film of water on your face into water vapor. This heat is taken from your skin, leaving it cooler.

AT START OF EXPERIMENT

COOLED WATER

MOIST TOWEL
TIGHTLY WRAPPED
AROUND BOTTLE

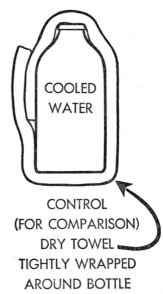

COOLED WATER

CONTROL
(FOR COMPARISON)
DRY TOWEL
TIGHTLY WRAPPED
AROUND BOTTLE

Can you use the same principle to keep a bottle or pitcher of drinking water cool on a warm summer day?

Set up two identical bottles of water which have been cooled in the refrigerator. Place them a few feet apart but where they will be subject to the same conditions of temperature, drafts, or shade.

Over one place a moist folded turkish towel which hugs the bottle. Wet the towel with tap water from time to time and wring it out. If the towel is too heavy to wring, use a lighter one.

Cover your control bottle with the same kind of towel but leave it dry.

Take temperatures of the water every twenty minutes. Try not to disturb the towels.

Record any condition—such as wind or nearness to

hot foods—that you think may have some bearing on the results.

Temperature of air at start of experiment	
Temperature of air at end of experiment	
Temperature of water used to wet towel	
Time experiment started	
Time experiment ended	

	Temperature of water at start	Temperature readings every 20 minutes
Bottle under moist towel		
Bottle under dry towel		

Is the temperature the same all over your home?

The thermometer in the living room indicates 70 degrees, yet your mother feels cold while your father says it is warm enough.

Of course, all people do not react alike to the same temperature, but can it be that there are different temperatures in the same room?

134

Find out, and while you are at it, do it for the entire house.

Make a sketch of the living room, dining room, and kitchen. Indicate windows, doors, radiators, and stairs.

Check your thermometer against a reliable one. You can still use yours, even if it does not check, by adding or subtracting the error for each reading.

Take every temperature reading at the same height from the floor. Do not keep your fingers on the bulb or even on the metal part of the thermometer.

It takes time for a thermometer to change, so wait until there is no further movement before you take a reading.

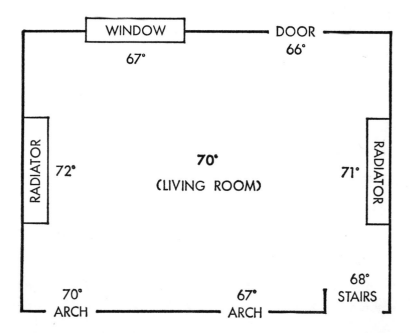

Write down the temperature on the drawings. Do the same for the basement, attic, and upstairs rooms.

Is the temperature the same at all levels in the room? In a heated room where there is no draft you may find a difference of five to fifteen degrees between the ceiling and the floor.

Make a chart showing the temperature in one room. If the ceiling is too high to reach by standing on a chair, tie the thermometer to a pole and hold it up to the ceiling on a slant.

More to find out:

How many hours a day is your refrigerator on?

How often does it go on during certain hours in the summer? In the winter? How long does it stay on? Include in your records how often the door is opened, also the outside temperature.

How many hours a day does your oil burner work?

Compare your findings with the outside temperature and also with the thermostat setting.

How long does water remain hot or cold in a vacuum bottle?

Take temperature readings every hour. Make a graph showing the loss of heat. Do the same for very cold

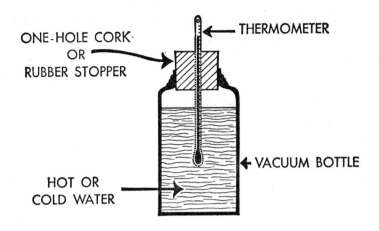

ONE-HOLE CORK·
OR
RUBBER STOPPER

THERMOMETER

VACUUM BOTTLE

HOT OR
COLD WATER

water. Does keeping the bottle in the hot sun or in the refrigerator make any difference? Set up the bottle as shown in the illustration.

What kind of natural stone is used in homes?

If you will look around you will discover places where marble, granite, slate, bluestone, shale, limestone, and many other stones are used for different purposes. Make a chart showing the locations and the special uses.

What is the strongest mixture of concrete?

Mix different amounts of cement, sand, and fine gravel. Make many 2-inch balls and allow them to harden. Drop each one from the same height onto a sidewalk. Record which balls break.

A good mixture is 1 part cement, 2 parts sand, and

2 parts fine gravel. Cover the drying mixture with a wet newspaper.

Books to read

Irving Adler, *Tools in Your Life,* New York: The John Day Company, Inc., 1956.

William A. Burns, *Man and His Tools,* New York: Whittlesey House, 1956.

Elizabeth K. Cooper, *Science in Your Own Back Yard,* New York: Harcourt, Brace and Company, Inc., 1958.

Herman Schneider, *Everyday Machines and How They Work*, New York: Whittlesey House, 1950.

Herbert S. Zim, *Things Around the House*, New York: William Morrow & Company, Inc., 1954.

Here are some good science books for more ideas

Nelson Beeler and Franklyn Branley, *Experiments in Science*, New York: Thomas Y. Crowell Company, 1955.

W. H. Crouse, *Understanding Science*, New York: Whittlesey House, 1956.

Joseph Leeming, *Real Book of Science Experiments*, New York: Garden City Books, 1954.

C. J. Lynde, *Science Experiments with Home Equipment*, Princeton, N.J.: D. Van Nostrand Company, Inc., 1949.

———, *Science Experiments with Inexpensive Equipment*, Princeton, N.J.: D. Van Nostrand Company, Inc., 1950.

Julius Schwartz, *It's Fun to Know Why*, New York: Whittlesey House, 1952.

K. M. Swezey, *After-Dinner Science*, New York: McGraw-Hill Book Company, Inc., 1948.

———, *Science Magic*, New York: McGraw-Hill Book Company, Inc., 1952.

INDEX

140

141